This book is presented to this child of God

....

From

....

On this day

....

To Luke,
a big kid and a man of God.
(Both are evidence of Christ in you.)
I've loved you since we were kids, and I'll love
you when we're old, wrinkly grown-ups too.
Thanks for being faithful and fun and
for pointing us to the Father.

Published in 2024 by B&H Publishing Group,
Brentwood, Tennessee.
Text copyright © 2024 by Caroline Saunders.
Illustrations copyright © 2024 by B&H Publishing Group.
ISBN: 978-1-4300-8353-5
Scripture quotations are taken from the Christian Standard Bible®,
Copyright © 2017 by Holman Bible Publishers.
Used by permission. Christian Standard Bible® and CSB® are
federally registered trademarks of Holman Bible Publishers.
Dewey Decimal Classification: C220.95
SUBHD: BIBLE STORIES / JESUS CHRIST
Printed in Shenzhen, Guangdong, China, November 2023
1 2 3 4 5 6 • 28 27 26 25 24

A Storybook Bible
About God's Children

Kids
in the
Bible

Caroline Saunders

Illustrations by Carlos Vélez Aguilera

B&H
kids

Nashville TN

A Note for Readers

Did you know the Bible is one big story about a Parent and children? Since God created everyone, He's like the Parent—and the "kids" He created are all over the Bible. Some of those kids are grown-ups who act like big babies and refuse to look to God as their Parent. Some are grown-ups who humbly know that on the inside, they're just kids who desperately need God to be their true Father. And some of the kids in the Bible are actual kids!

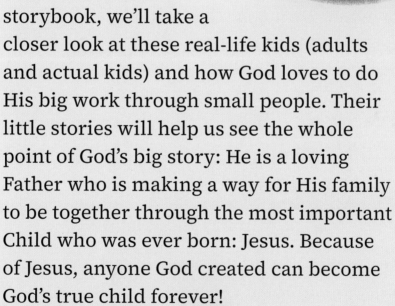

Kids are a part of God's special plan to bless the whole world. In this Bible storybook, we'll take a closer look at these real-life kids (adults and actual kids) and how God loves to do His big work through small people. Their little stories will help us see the whole point of God's big story: He is a loving Father who is making a way for His family to be together through the most important Child who was ever born: Jesus. Because of Jesus, anyone God created can become God's true child forever!

Contents

1. The Good Parent and the Good Garden 9

2. The Rescuer Boy (and the Spare) 16

3. Abraham's Impossible Family 23

4. Two Sons and a Sacrifice 28

5. The Colorful Coat and the Jealous Brothers 34

6. The Brave Sister and the Basket Baby 40

7. The Wilderness Kids 47

8. The Strong Guy 52

9. The Little Priest 59

10. Fearfully and Wonderfully Made 64

11. The Warrior Kid 70

12. The King Who Was Hungry for Wisdom 76

13. Kids Who Grow in Wisdom 81

14. The Twice-Saved Boy 84

15. The Good News Girl 91

16. The Kid King 96

17. The Little King Who Loved God's Law 100

18. God's Carefully Planned Prophet 107

19. Brave in the Blaze 112

20. The Brave and Beautiful Queen 119

21. The Promised Child Is Coming! 126

22. The Baby Messenger 132

23. The Change-the-World-Forever Baby 138

24. The Son in the Father's House 148

25. The Growing Family 155

26. The Miracle Meal 160

27. Jesus Loves Kids 169

28. The Get-Better Boy and the Live-Again Girl 174

29. The Cross: Where God the Father Gave
    and God the Son Stayed 180

30. He Is Alive! 186

31. Planting Seeds and Growing Kids 193

32. We Are God's Children 198

33. Good News for God's Kids 205

The Story of the Child 210

Am I a Child of God? 216

Now What? 219

Your Story of Being God's Kid 220

I'm God's Kid! 222

1

The Good Parent and the Good Garden

Genesis 1–3

In the beginning, there was nothing—until God created everything. God said, "Let there be light," and BOOM! There was light. Whatever God told to "be" would immediately "be." Pretty amazing, huh?

As a grand finale, God made His most treasured creation: people. Adam and Eve were grown-ups, but they were still God's children. Everything was new to them in the special garden-home God had made. As a good parent, God helped them live, work, and play. God said people were made in His image, which meant no part of creation was as much like God as they were. This was God's idea: Adam and Eve would have kids, their kids would have kids, then their kids would have kids—and pretty soon, the world would be full of God's image-bearing kids! It was a wonderful idea. God loves kids!

Adam and Eve would look like their Father, and He would teach His kids to rely on Him to give them anything they would ever need. Under God's care, Adam and Eve would learn more about their Father, follow His teaching, and grow on the outside and on the inside! As they walked with God, who is wise, they would become wise. (A wise person is someone who knows God's ideas and understands how to act on them.)

That's why God made a rule in His new creation: Adam and Eve should not eat from the tree called the tree of knowledge of good and bad. (Adam and Eve didn't need a tree to grow in wisdom and learn about good and bad. God would teach them!)

But one day—*hisssss*—a serpent came. This wasn't an ordinary snake like you might see at the zoo or in your friend's terrarium. Instead, he talked—and Adam and Eve listened! They didn't squeal and run away, the way some of us do when we spot a creepy creature. They talked with him. They didn't know he was an expert at lying, and that his words were a trap door to terribleness.

You see, this serpent hated God. He wanted to destroy God's treasured creation. The Bible gives the serpent a few names you might recognize like Satan, the Accuser, and the Father of Lies.

The serpent asked Eve, "Did God really say, 'You can't eat from any tree in the garden'?" That wasn't true! God had given Adam and Eve tons of delicious fruit trees. Their home was a snack factory! Eve corrected the serpent, telling him only one tree was off-limits. Adam had told Eve what God said, so Eve tried to tell the serpent, "God said, 'You must not eat it or touch it, or you will die.'"

Eve didn't get the rule totally right—God never said anything to Adam about touching the tree—but remember she was kind of like a kid! She was still growing.

The serpent knew she was still growing, and he used it as a weapon against her. He said, "You will not die!" Instead, he told her that eating from the tree would make her wise. Eve wanted to be wise! But does wisdom come from a tree or from God?

God's children had no reason to trust this serpent and every reason to trust God, but Eve still reached for the fruit and ate it. And Adam took a bite too. They wanted wisdom, but they didn't want to get it God's way. They took the shortcut, realizing too late it was a trap.

When Adam and Eve made this choice, they sinned. Sin is when we don't believe God's ideas are good and step outside of them. Sin always leads to death. It's as sneaky as a snake, seeming to be a good thing at first and then turning poisonous. As soon as sin entered the world that day in the garden, everything went wonky. And when Adam and Eve heard God coming, they hid.

Sometimes kids hide from their parents to be silly, but this wasn't a game. Adam and Eve were full of shame (that icky, horrible feeling when you know you've messed up), and they were full of blame (that thing we do when we pretend our mistake is someone else's fault). Yes, the serpent tricked Adam and Eve, but the sin was Adam and Eve's fault. They had not trusted their Father.

As a loving Parent, God told Adam and Eve the consequences: He had designed everything to be life-giving, but things would now be different with sin in the world. Work, growing a family, and relationships would all be frustrating and painful. Even so, there was good news: one day a Child would be born, and He would defeat that sneaky serpent forever. **This Child was God's special plan to bless the whole world.**

Dear God,

You are a loving Father. Grow me in wisdom so I can follow Your words no matter what! Amen.

2
The Rescuer Boy (and the Spare)
Genesis 4

Adam and Eve became parents. With every baby Eve had, maybe she looked for the Child God had promised. Who would be the one to set the world right again? (Maybe you can be looking for that as you read this book!)

You probably know that the names mothers and fathers give their children are important and special. (Does your name have a special meaning?)

First, Eve had a baby named Cain. When she chose this name, she said, "I have had a boy with the Lord's help." Maybe the name was a way for Eve to praise God, or maybe Eve hoped Cain was the promised Child who would rescue her family.

Soon, Eve gave birth to a second son, Abel. Abel's name is kind of like the Hebrew word for "worthless." If Adam and Eve were counting on Cain to be the rescuer boy, maybe they felt that Abel was like a spare tire. When the main tires are doing great, a spare tire is not very important.

Maybe it was hard for Cain and Abel to grow up with these names. Cain might've believed that rescuing the world was on his shoulders, and Abel might've been unsure he had any purpose at all. Whatever life was like for these kids, we know it wasn't perfect like it was in Eden. We know they were in need of God's rescue through the Child promised by God.

One day when they were grown, Cain and Abel both gave offerings, which are gifts given to worship God. But God wasn't okay with Cain's offering because Cain offered it with a mean and selfish heart.

Abel's offering, though, made God so happy! That must have made Abel's heart soar. Even though other people might have thought he was unimportant, God loved him. Maybe Abel did a cartwheel or twirled around until he got so dizzy that he fell down. Being loved by God is the best thing ever!

But Cain was angry. Maybe he thought, *I'm the better brother! Why doesn't God know that?*

Cain wasn't just angry with God—he was angry toward his brother. After all, Abel had something Cain didn't have: God's favor. This kind of anger is called envy, and envy is a sin. Sin is when we think, *My ideas are better than God's ideas. I'm going to do what I want instead of what He wants.* Sin always leads to death.

Think about it: God has designed brothers (and sisters) to love and serve one another, but how can they do that when one brother is full of anger toward the other and wants what his brother has? Envy might seem like a "no big deal" sin, but all sin is a big deal! All sin is dangerous.

God knew the danger and warned Cain. God said, "Your sin is like a hungry tiger, and it is going to gobble you up. You need to destroy it!"

But instead of listening to God's wisdom and attacking the sin of envy, Cain fed his envy and let it grow. One terrible day, Cain attacked his brother, Abel.

God said, "Cain, what have you done?!" This is not what brothers should do. Brothers should keep one another safe, but now Abel was dead.

All hope seemed to be dead too! After all, Cain wasn't a rescuer—he was a destroyer. What hope was there for rescue?

But God always keeps His promises. Terribleness can seem like the end of the story, but it never is. It means God is not done working.

Soon Eve had another son, Seth, and she felt hope again. **Seth was just a kid—but he was part of God's special plan to bless the whole world.** One day, the promised Child would come through Seth's family, and the true Rescuer Boy would make a way for enemies to become family.

Dear God,

I can see that even "little" sins are a big deal. I need Your rescue! Help me to love Your wisdom rather than trusting in my own. Amen.

3

Abraham's Impossible Family

Genesis 12; 16–18; 21:1–7

The whole world seemed cursed, so it was a big deal when God chose a man named Abraham and gave him a promise: "I am going to give you a big family, and I will bless the whole world through this family!" Abraham was surprised to hear this promise. He didn't have any kids, and he was already the age of a grandpa: seventy-five years old! It might have seemed crazy, but Abraham knew God could do anything. So Abraham trusted Him.

Ten years went by, and there was still no baby. Abraham's wife, Sarah, had an idea: Abraham should have a baby with another woman, Hagar. Hagar was younger and able to have children. Plus, she worked for Abraham and Sarah and had to do whatever they said. This was a terrible idea for lots of reasons. For one, Abraham and Sarah didn't seem to care what Hagar thought. They treated her like a thing instead of a person! Two, Abraham was supposed to have a baby only with his wife, Sarah. And three, Abraham and Sarah must've forgotten that God can do anything. They were following their own ideas instead of God's ideas.

But Abraham and Sarah thought they could create God's promised family themselves, so they put Sarah's plan into action. When Hagar became pregnant, she looked at Sarah with hate, so Sarah mistreated her. When the mistreatment became too much, Hagar ran away into the desert.

In this impossible place, something amazing happened! God met Hagar and told her about the plans He had for her baby. You see, God sees a child and knows everything about him or her even before the child's parents have seen his or her face! (After all, God is the one who makes all children.) God even told Hagar to name her son Ishmael, which means "God hears."

Comfort filled Hagar's heart. Although Abraham and Sarah didn't see Hagar as a person, God saw her and her child. They mattered to God! Worshiping God, Hagar called Him "El-roi," which means, "You are the God who sees me." God's love for her and her son gave Hagar the courage to listen to God when He asked her to return to Abraham and Sarah.

Soon, Hagar gave birth to Ishmael. His father, Abraham, was . . . wait for it . . . eighty-six years old. Every time Hagar held Ishmael or called his name, it was a reminder: God hears. God sees.

Even though God created, saw, and knew Ishmael, this child was not the way God would fulfill His promise to Abraham. God wanted to fulfill His promise in an impossible way so that when people saw it, they would say, "Whoa! Only God could do that!"

When Abraham was almost one hundred years old and Sarah was ninety, God reminded Abraham of His promise: "Sarah is going to have a child, and you will name him Isaac."

Isaac means "he laughs," probably because the whole thing was pretty funny! Who ever heard of a nearly hundred-year-old couple having a baby? Sarah laughed when she heard the news, but not in a happy way. She laughed with a mean spirit, like, "Yeah, right! God can't do that. We are the wrinkly-est, oldest people in the world. What nonsense."

It did seem like nonsense because it made no sense! But God loves to do what makes no sense to us. (That's how we know He did it and not us. And it's really fun when the things that made no sense start to make perfect sense, and we jump up and down and say, "Look what God did! He is amazing!")

The next year, even though it seemed impossible, Sarah gave birth to Isaac. Sarah laughed again, but this time with joy. As she rocked this impossible little boy in her old-lady arms, she bubbled over with delight, knowing that nothing is impossible for God! **Isaac was just a kid, but he was part of God's special plan to bless the whole world.**

Dear God,

I am so glad that You can do the impossible! Thank You for being awesome. Amen.

4

Two Sons and a Sacrifice

Genesis 21–22

When a baby is born, it can feel like a happy ending. But of course, birth is just a beginning. Isaac's birth made everyone giggle with joy, but this joy was often under attack.

One day, Abraham and Hagar's son Ishmael, who was now a teenager, made fun of young Isaac. Sarah was furious! She demanded Abraham force Hagar and Ishmael to leave forever.

Abraham did not want to lose his first son! However, God comforted him: "I will keep My promise to you through Isaac, and I will also bless your son Ishmael." Sarah's demand was unkind, but God promised to bring good from this terribleness. Abraham decided to trust God. He packed food and water for Hagar and Ishmael and said a sad goodbye.

The two outcasts headed into the wilderness. Eventually, their food and water ran out, and Hagar cried, worried her son would die. Yes, Ishmael looked like a grown-up compared to little Isaac, but he was still a kid! How could they possibly survive? Once again, God met Hagar, and He reminded her that she and Ishmael were seen, heard, and under His care. No matter where they went, God was in charge. He would keep His promise to bless Ishmael.

God provided for them that day and every day after that as Hagar raised Ishmael in the wilderness. The desert once felt like, well, a desert. But now it felt like *dessert* because God was with them!

Back at Abraham's home, Isaac continued to grow. One day, God asked Abraham to do an impossible thing—the hardest thing a father could imagine. God said, "I want you to offer Isaac as a sacrifice."

When people offered a sacrifice, they put an animal to death to show what sin deserves. Offering a sacrifice was a way for people to say to God: "I agree with You that my sin is a big deal."

Abraham had placed animals upon altars many times before. But now, God was asking Abraham to do a new and impossible thing: place his precious, promised son Isaac upon the altar and offer him as a sacrifice!

Why would God ask Abraham to do something like this? When we have big questions, it's wise to remember what God is like. Abraham knew God is good, and he knew God can do the impossible. He decided, "God is powerful enough to raise Isaac from the dead. I can trust God, so I will follow Him no matter what." Imagine how much faith Abraham had in God!

He woke up early; gathered his son, servants, and animals; split firewood; journeyed to the place God said; and finally, walked with his beloved son to the altar.

Isaac had made sacrifices with his father before, but this time was different. "Daddy, where is the lamb for the offering?" Isaac asked. Isaac's name means "he laughs," but no one was laughing that day.

In faith, Abraham replied, "God will provide."
In faith, Abraham placed Isaac on the altar.
In faith, Abraham picked up the knife.

But then he heard a voice. "Abraham! Do not lay a hand on the boy! Now I know that you trust and worship God with your whole heart." When Abraham looked up, he spotted a ram that could be offered on the altar instead of Isaac. A scary, dark day ended with great gladness: God provided the offering. God can be trusted.

Isaac was just a kid—but he was forever part of God's special plan to bless the whole world, and God never breaks His promises.

Dear God,
Thank You for keeping Your
promises. Help me to trust You
even when I can't understand
what You're doing.
Amen.

5

The Colorful Coat
and the Jealous Brothers

Genesis 37; 39–47

Remember what God promised Abraham? He said, "I am going to give you a big family, and I will bless the whole world through this family!" That promise didn't make sense until Isaac was born, and then it made more sense when Isaac grew up to have twins, Jacob and Esau. When Jacob grew up, he had thirteen kids: twelve sons and one daughter. Whoa—that's a lot of children! God's seemingly impossible promise of a big family was slowly coming true.

But what about the other part of the promise? How would this family be a blessing? After all, like every family, Jacob's family had troubles. Families are supposed to love one another, but most of Jacob's sons hated one of the youngest brothers, Joseph. Joseph was their dad's favorite. Jacob even made Joseph a special, colorful robe, but none of the other brothers got one. It wasn't fair! Standing in their boring brown robes next to crayon-colored Joseph, the brothers couldn't forget their dad was a favorite-picker.

To make things worse, Joseph dreamt about his brothers bowing down to him, and he blabbed those dreams to his brothers as they worked together as shepherds. Envy began to grow in the brothers' hearts—that mean feeling that says, "I want to take what you have." This sin grew and grew, like it wanted to gobble the brothers up.

When Joseph was seventeen years old, his jealous brothers had an idea—one that seemed good to them but was actually poisonous. They thought, "Let's kill him!" To them, Joseph was just a thing that kept their father from loving them more.

One brother, Reuben, stood up for Joseph and said, "Don't kill him! Let's just throw him into this pit." Reuben was secretly planning to rescue Joseph later.

But when Reuben returned, he learned his brothers had sold Joseph to some passing travelers for twenty pieces of silver. Because of these mean brothers, Joseph would soon become a slave in Egypt! The rest of the brothers weren't sorry, but Reuben was devastated. What would their father say?

To keep from telling their father the evil truth, the brothers crafted a lie. They took Joseph's special coat—the one their father had given him—and covered it in goat's blood. They took it to their father, making him believe that a wild animal had devoured Joseph. It never occurred to Jacob that sin had devoured his other sons or that Joseph, at just seventeen years old, would soon be a slave in Egypt.

Things weren't easy for Joseph in Egypt, but God was with him. **Joseph was just a kid, but he—and his brothers, as hateful as they were—were part of God's special plan to bless the whole world.**

Joseph spent time enslaved and in jail, but no matter where he was, people trusted him. They knew he was special. It wasn't a coat that made Joseph special—it was the way God the Father covered him with wisdom. As Joseph trusted God more, he became wiser!

Eventually, Joseph helped the ruler of Egypt, Pharaoh, see that the land would soon face a terrible famine. (That's a time when there isn't enough food to feed people.) Joseph had a wise plan to protect people, so Pharaoh put him in charge of everything.

When the famine spread all the way back to Jacob's home, Joseph's brothers heard about a wise man with food in Egypt. They packed up and headed that way. When they arrived, Joseph was startled to see his brothers bowing down to him and asking for help!

Of course, the brothers didn't recognize him. How could they have ever imagined this powerful man was the kid brother they had betrayed? Not only had Joseph grown on the outside, but he'd grown on the inside too. When he revealed himself to his brothers, they were terrified he would kill them. But Joseph said, "Your plan was evil, but God used it for good."

Joseph trusted God, and like God, he offered kindness to his brothers. He invited them and their father to come live in Egypt, where Joseph could take care of them.

Dear God,
I know that I will grow
on the inside as I learn
to trust You, like Joseph.
Will You help me?
Amen.

6

The Brave Sister
and the Basket Baby

Exodus 1:1–2:10

Joseph and his brothers had kids, and their kids had kids. Soon, Egypt was jam-packed with thousands of families that had grown from all those sons of Jacob! In fact, there were so many of them that it started to get on the new Pharaoh's nerves. He worried the kids would grow up and take over. To protect himself, he did two horrible things. First, he forced this nation of families to work as slaves. That means they didn't have a choice, they didn't get paid, and they weren't treated like people. (Pharaoh probably figured if they were busy working, they wouldn't have the energy to overthrow him.) Second, Pharaoh commanded that all their baby boys should be thrown into the Nile River. He didn't want even one of them to grow up to be a strong leader.

It was a scary time to be a kid in this family! But you know what? Even though they were probably afraid, this family showed great courage.

First, there were the brave midwives. Midwives are women who help other women give birth. These midwives didn't obey Pharaoh. They let the baby boys live! Their courage made God very glad, and He blessed them.

Second, there were brave parents. One couple looked at their baby boy and knew he was fearfully and wonderfully made, so they hid him away.

Third, there was the baby's brave sister, Miriam. When her parents couldn't hide her little brother any longer, her mom did something unusual: she placed the baby in a basket, and she tucked the basket into the reeds at the bank of the Nile River. Miriam stood close by to see what would happen. It was very courageous of her, but sisters tend to be brave when it comes to their siblings.

You won't believe who found the baby—Pharaoh's daughter! She was a rich and powerful princess, but when she saw the crying baby, she felt compassion. (If you've ever seen a friend get hurt, and you run toward them to help, that's compassion. Compassion invites us to have courage to help someone.)

Brave Miriam walked up to Pharaoh's daughter. Even though Miriam was young, she was growing in wisdom, and even though she was supposed to act like a slave, she was brave and bold. Miriam said to Pharaoh's daughter, "Would you like me to find a woman who can take care of this baby for you?"

Perhaps Pharaoh's daughter had already decided to raise this baby herself, or perhaps Miriam's suggestion planted that idea in her mind. Either way, compassion invited the princess to have courage. Instead of obeying her father and having this baby put to death, she decided to treat this baby as her own. She agreed to Miriam's plan, saying, "Take this child and take care of him for me, and I will pay you."

Miriam must have been so glad to gather her baby brother into her arms and run home. Of course Miriam knew the perfect woman to take care of this baby—their mother!

When the baby boy was no longer a baby, his mom took him to Pharaoh's daughter, and he became her son. The princess named him Moses.

Even though Miriam and her mother were grateful Moses's life was safe, it probably was still a very sad day for them. But a sad day means God is not done working. Yes, this boy would be raised in Egypt, but when Moses was grown, God would use him to rescue His people.

Not only that, but God would also use Moses's education to help him write the first five books of the Bible! Most importantly, God would use Moses's story to point to another Child who would come and rescue God's people from something worse: the slavery of sin. **Moses was just a kid, but he was part of God's special plan to bless the whole world.**

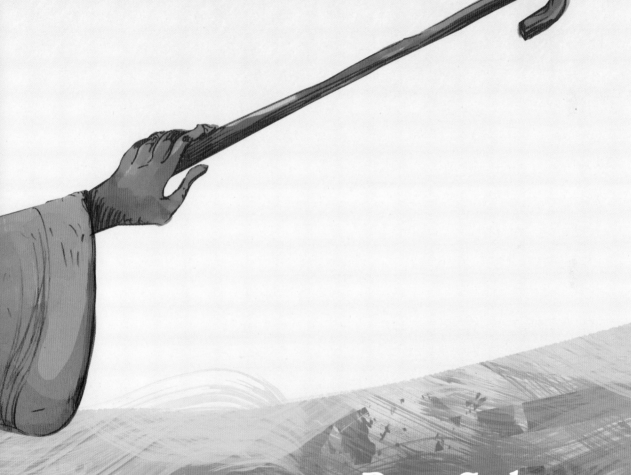

Dear God,

Thank You for these examples of bravery in the Bible. As I grow, grow me in courage! Amen.

7

The Wilderness Kids

Deuteronomy 6; Numbers 14

Remember the big, big family that had become Pharaoh's slaves? When Moses grew older, God used Moses to rescue them. This family, all from the twelve sons of Jacob, was now twelve tribes that added up to lots and lots of people—and they were all finally free!

God named this big family Israel. He promised He would bring them home to a special place He had picked out for them, a place "flowing with milk and honey." That doesn't mean milk and honey rivers. It means the Promised Land was a place with lush green pastures, clean water, and beautiful flowers—everything cows or goats need to make tons of milk and everything bees need to make tons of honey! The Israelites couldn't wait to get home. But on the way, the grown-ups got really grumbly. They were like kids on a road trip, whining, "Are we there yet?"—except worse! They said things like, "Why did God rescue us from Egypt if He's just going to let us die in the wilderness?" They acted like they didn't know God at all!

The people in the big family had a sin problem. (Remember, sin is when we don't believe God's ideas are good and we step outside of them.) This sin problem got even clearer as the people got closer to the home God had promised. Some of their men went to peek at the land, and they got scared because they saw giant warriors living there. The people said, "God's plan will put our children in danger! Why has God brought us here?" They had totally forgotten how powerful God is, how He'd rescued them from Egypt, and how much God loves children!

As a consequence of their sin, and to help the people grow to truly know Him, God didn't let them go home. None of the grown-ups who distrusted God would get to live in the Promised Land. They would live the rest of their days in the wilderness, and after they died, their kids—the ones they mistakenly believed God would harm—would experience the wonderfulness of this home. That meant this big family had to hang out in the wilderness for forty years. Imagine how many times they asked, "Are we there yet?" on that never-ending road trip!

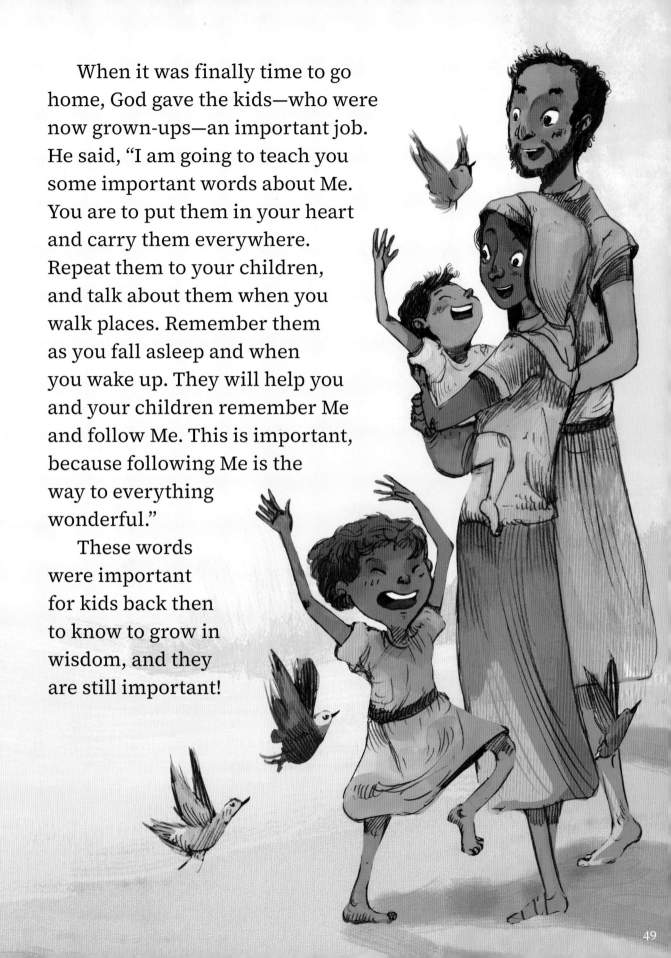

When it was finally time to go home, God gave the kids—who were now grown-ups—an important job. He said, "I am going to teach you some important words about Me. You are to put them in your heart and carry them everywhere. Repeat them to your children, and talk about them when you walk places. Remember them as you fall asleep and when you wake up. They will help you and your children remember Me and follow Me. This is important, because following Me is the way to everything wonderful."

These words were important for kids back then to know to grow in wisdom, and they are still important!

So pay close attention to the words:

Listen, Israel:
*The L*ORD *our God, the L*ORD *is one.*
*Love the L*ORD *your God with all your heart,*
with all your soul,
and with all your strength.
—Deuteronomy 6:4–5

If the kids remembered these words, they would grow up knowing that God is most important and that they could love Him with all they have. They would grow up in the home God had promised—the one flowing with milk and honey—and their big family would form a nation that pointed the whole world to follow God. After all, following God is the way to everything wonderful. **Yes, the Israelites were just kids, but they were part of God's special plan to bless the whole world.**

Dear God,

I know You are the way to everything wonderful. Help me to love You with all my heart, soul, and strength. Amen.

8
The Strong Guy

Judges 13–16

The twelve tribes of Israel grew, but they didn't always love God with all their heart, soul, and strength. They often were determined not to let God be in charge. Finally, God let the Philistines be in charge of them instead. The Philistines and Israelites fought a lot. The Israelites did not like being bossed around!

But God was committed to His people, so He did something about their pain: He sent a baby who would grow to rescue them. The world doesn't usually look at babies like rescuers, but God loves to give children His strength so they can grow in wisdom and point the world toward Him.

God had a special plan, and it started with a woman who had been unable to have any children. Remember, nothing is impossible with God! God's angel gave the woman exciting news: "You are going to have a son. This son will be special." As a sign to the world that her son was specially sent from God as a rescuer, God told the woman not to drink certain drinks or eat certain foods. He also told her never to cut her son's hair.

The woman told her husband what God said, and he prayed a wise prayer: "God, teach us everything we should do to raise this child." God loves when His children ask for wisdom! And He loves when parents want to raise their children with wisdom! God sent His angel, who taught them more about God and about the child who was coming.

Soon, the woman gave birth to a son, and she named him Samson. As Samson grew, God blessed him, and God's Spirit began to whoosh within him, showing Samson how to be a rescuer. **Samson was just a kid, but he was part of God's special plan to bless the whole world!**

And Samson did a lot of rescuing. He grew up to be a judge of God's people, which is like a ruler—and he was a very strong ruler. He was the strongest man anyone had ever met, with strength so amazing that people knew it was from God! Because of God, Samson became mighty. He fought a lion and won. He also defeated Israel's enemy, the mean Philistines, in battle after battle. If there were a "Strongest Dude" contest, Samson definitely would have won.

But Samson did not love God with all his heart, soul, and strength. He loved women. One woman named Delilah knew Samson loved her more than God, and when the Philistines offered to pay her to trick Samson, she did. You see, when we give God our heart, soul, and strength, we are safe, because He loves us no matter what. But when we give our heart, soul, and strength to people, we aren't living with wisdom. Samson told Delilah the rule about his hair, so when he was asleep, Delilah cut it. When he woke up, his strength had melted like ice cream in a microwave. God's Spirit had left him! Samson forgot it was God who made him strong—and the Philistines captured him.

The Philistines treated Samson terribly and put him in prison. At a big party where they were worshipping their fake god Dagon, they brought Samson out to laugh at him. In their minds, because Samson was weak, God was weak, and their fake god was strong. But Samson prayed God would strengthen him one last time, and God did! Samson shoved the pillars of the building over, and it all tumbled down on top of everyone in one big, terrible heap. It was proof that God is the one true God!

Samson's story ends with a big, jumbly crash. Yes, baby Samson grew up to rescue God's people, but the world was still such a mess! But there was good news: One day, God would send another baby boy who would bless the whole world. He would die, too, but it wouldn't be the end of His story.

Dear God,

I know You are the safest place for my heart, soul, and strength. Help me never to forget that You are the One who makes me strong. Amen.

9
The Little Priest
1 Samuel 1–3

For a while, God's people were led by judges, like Samson, and by priests, like a man named Eli. Eli's job was to connect God and His people. It was an important job, and God wanted priests to take their job seriously.

One day, Eli saw a woman named Hannah in the temple. She was moving her mouth without talking, and it seemed strange! To Eli, it looked like she was up to no good. But Hannah was simply praying in her heart because she was desperate to have a child. She told God, "Please see me! If You will let me have a child, I will give him to You forever. He will be set apart to serve You."

Eli looked down on the woman and told her to act better. When she explained she was praying and brokenhearted, the strangeness finally made sense to Eli. God was at work! He said, "May God give you what you've asked for."

Guess what? God did! Hannah had a baby boy. She named him Samuel, which kind of sounds like the Hebrew phrase for "I asked God." After a few years, Hannah took Samuel to Eli at the temple. She said, "Remember me? I am the woman who was praying and brokenhearted, but look! God answered my prayer. I am giving my precious little boy to God so that he can serve God all his life." Little Samuel began to live with Eli in the temple to learn how to be a priest.

Eli's sons were priests, too, but they didn't take this important job seriously. Rather than serving the people, Eli's sons made God's people serve them. Eli didn't seem to care.

Finally, it was time for God to act. In the middle of the night, God called to Samuel. **Samuel was just a kid, but he was part of God's special plan to bless the whole world!**

God said, "Samuel!" The little boy had never heard from God before, so he thought Eli was calling him. He popped out of bed, ran to Eli, and said, "Here I am!" Sleepy and confused, Eli quickly sent the boy to bed.

Again God called, "Samuel!" Samuel ran to Eli a second time, saying, "Here I am!" Eli rubbed his tired eyes and sent Samuel back to bed. Eli was probably thinking, *What's the deal with this kid? Can't an old priest get any sleep around here?*

Samuel heard the voice a third time, and that's when the strangeness finally made sense to Eli. God was at work! God was calling Samuel!

Samuel didn't really know God yet, but it was time. Eli told Samuel, "God is calling you. When He calls again, say, 'Speak, Lord, for Your servant is listening.'" Samuel did as Eli told him, and God began to tell Samuel His plan. Eli and his sons would no longer be priests, and they would be punished for how they had misused their important job.

God's plan seemed like bad news, so Samuel was afraid to share it with Eli. But when Eli asked him, Samuel showed courage and told the truth. (He would have to do that very thing hundreds more times in his life as he served the Lord.) Yes, it sounded like bad news, but Eli responded in faith: "The Lord is the Lord. Let Him do what He thinks is good."

Young Samuel grew, and God was with him. God did all that He said He would do. Eli and his sons died, and Samuel served God as a priest. God asked Samuel to do lots of important work that required wisdom and courage, and Samuel took it seriously, helping others to truly know and follow God. Samuel did his best to love God with all his heart, soul, and strength. He wasn't perfect, but he was part of God's special plan to bless the whole world.

Dear God,

Help me to listen when You want to speak to me through Your Word, the Bible. Help me to take the work You ask me to do seriously. Amen.

10
Fearfully and Wonderfully Made
1 Samuel 16; Psalm 139

Sometimes we feel like we're *too* different from other people. Other times we wish we could be *more* like someone else. As humans, it's easy to feel unsure about the way God made us! Around the time of Samuel, God's people were feeling the same way.

The Israelites were tired of being different from the nearby nations, who had kings. They wanted a king too! It didn't matter to them that being different was God's idea for them, and it didn't matter that God told them a king would be bad for them. They didn't care about God's idea or think it was good. So God gave them what they wanted.

Their first king was a guy named Saul, and he looked the way you'd expect a king to look—tall and handsome. If there were an award for "Most King-Looking Dude," Saul would have won. But there was a problem: Saul didn't love the Lord with all his heart, mind, and strength. Instead, he loved himself.

God told Samuel, who was now a grown-up priest and judge, that He had chosen a new king to replace Saul. God brought Samuel to a family with lots of sons. Samuel thought God would pick one of the older brothers since they looked kingly. But God made it clear that He'd chosen the youngest, a boy named David. It didn't make sense to Samuel (or to David's family), but God was clear: "I don't look at the outside—I look at the heart." God made this boy's heart, and He knew this boy would try to love Him with all of it.

David once wrote a song about how God made him. He wrote it in a different language than ours (Hebrew), but it went something like this:

You created all of me—even those parts
deep inside no one sees.
You knit me together in my mother's womb.
I praise You and clap and cheer for You
because I am fearfully made—
the way You made me makes me worship You,
because I am wonderfully made—
the way You made me is delightfully different from others!
Everything You make is wonderful, and I am sure about that.
Before anyone kissed my face or knew my name, You saw me.
Even then, You had every day of my life
written in Your book.

David's story and David's song have lots of good news for children . . .

- God sees, knows, and loves us before we are born.

- God made us, and the way He made us invites us to praise Him.

- God made us, and He made our differences on purpose.

- God has every day of our lives written down way before they ever happen.

Children are a miracle! Think about it:

How do your lungs know to breathe in and out even when you're sleeping?

How does your heart know to beat?

How does your body heal that scrape on your knee in just a few days?

Why do your tastebuds get so excited when you get to chomp on a cheesy piece of pizza?

Why does your nose make a happy "sniff-sniff" when something smells like Christmas?

God did all of that! Thank You, God!

When you feel unloved or unseen, it's wise and wonderful to remember that God loves you and sees you, just like He saw David. When you feel different from others, it's wise and wonderful to remember that God designed you to be distinct. When you feel like life is out of control, it's wise and wonderful to remember that God has all your days written down.

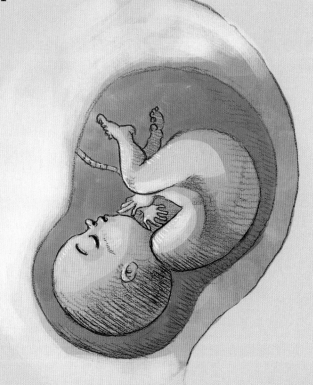

Think about it: David wrote that song about three thousand years ago, but right now, you get to be blessed by it! **David was just a kid, but he was part of God's special plan to bless the whole world.** You are just a kid, but you, too, are part of God's special plan to bless the whole world!

Dear God,

Help me to praise You because I am fearfully and wonderfully made. Thank You for seeing me!
Amen.

11

The Warrior Kid

1 Samuel 17; Psalm 23; John 10

Sometimes we want to speed up time and skip to more fun stuff. Maybe you want a vacation to start soon. Maybe you want to hurry up and be a grown-up. Maybe you want the school day to whoosh past so you can get home and play!

David probably felt like that. Samuel had anointed him king, but it wasn't God's time for David to rule yet. All he could do was wait—and seek to love God with all his heart, mind, and strength, even on the boring days.

But one day was pretty exciting.

David's older brothers had joined other Israelites and King Saul to fight their enemy, the Philistines. Well, they were *supposed* to be fighting, but the battle had frozen. A giant Philistine warrior named Goliath had threatened God's people, demanding someone come fight him. Everyone was terrified because this guy looked taller and mightier than any guy they'd ever seen! He seemed really grumpy, too, like someone had woken him up by plucking out his beard. The Israelites' courage melted like warm butter.

Speaking of butter, David went to the battlefield to deliver food to his brothers. When David heard the warrior's threats, he was mad! David thought, *Who is this guy who thinks he can threaten God's people? Doesn't he know God is with us?*

On all those boring days, God had been growing courage in David. David was a shepherd, so his job was to keep his sheep safe and full of life. When bears and lions tried to attack David's flock, David bravely fought and killed them. Now that David saw God's people under attack, his shepherding instincts kicked in. David would do whatever it took to keep God's sheep safe and thriving. So what if Goliath was a giant? David had God on his side! **David was just a kid, but he was part of God's special plan to bless the whole world.**

David's bravery annoyed his brothers, and it made no sense to King Saul. But King Saul agreed to let David face Goliath. He even let David try on the kingly armor! The armor didn't fit, so David went as himself, knowing God was the best armor in the world. He also grabbed a few stones from a nearby stream and put them in his shepherd's pouch.

When Goliath saw young David, he immediately hated him. He must have thought, *How rude for the Israelites to send this puny kid when they know I'm a mighty warrior!*

But David stood in courage. He shouted to Goliath, "You come against me with weapons, but I come against you in the name of the Lord!" (Goliath had no idea what a mighty weapon that is.)

David continued, "When I defeat you, it'll prove to everyone that God saves, and every battle belongs to Him." Goliath ran to attack, but David grabbed one of the stones from his bag, put it in his slingshot, and slung it toward Goliath. *THWAP!* The stone sunk into Goliath's forehead. *THUNK!* The fierce warrior fell to the ground.

Whenever anyone heard the story of the young boy who defeated the fearsome giant with just a stone, it made no sense! They could only think one thing: "God did this!"

David was a courageous shepherd boy that exciting day because he was shepherded by God. David once wrote a song about that. It starts like this: "The Lord is my shepherd." David knew God was with him always, helping him grow and thrive on boring days and exciting days, guiding him through scary times, caring for him when

enemies hated him, and promising to bring him home one day. Because God was David's Shepherd, David could face bears, lions, and even giant, terrifying warriors.

God's children have sung David's shepherd song for centuries! In fact, a thousand years later, a man named Jesus talked about David's shepherd song. He said, "I am the Good Shepherd." Can you believe it? David's song was about Him—Jesus! Jesus is God, and He came to the battlefield of earth to defeat an enemy much scarier than Goliath: our sin. He would do whatever it took to protect us, God's sheep.

Dear God,

You are my shepherd. I know You are with me always. Help me remember. Amen.

12
The King Who Was Hungry for Wisdom
1 Kings 3–11

When he was old, King David gave his throne to his young son, Solomon. This was strange because Solomon had older brothers who probably seemed more "kingly." But David knew the Lord loves to do His big work through smallish people. Solomon wasn't technically a kid, but he felt like a kid. Sometimes grown-ups feel like little kids on the inside. It must have been scary for Solomon to think about leading a whole kingdom!

Besides running God's kingdom, Solomon was given a super important job: to build a special temple that would be considered the Lord's house forever. Before King David died, he told the whole kingdom about the plan, saying, "God has chosen my son Solomon to lead, though he is young and inexperienced."

Solomon might've thought, *Wow. Thanks, Dad, for reminding everyone that I'm totally not prepared for this job!* How was this brand-new, barely-a-grown-up king going to do the big job of leading God's people and building God's house? He probably felt like a kindergartener who'd been accidentally elected president!

One night, God talked to young Solomon in a dream and asked him, "What do you want me to give you?" Solomon could've asked for money, a long life, fame, unlimited cheeseburgers—*anything*—but he didn't. He said, "Lord, You have made me king, but I am so young! I don't know what I'm doing. Will You give me wisdom? Your wisdom will help me see the difference between good and bad so that I can lead Your people well."

God was so happy to hear this! Parents love it when their children are hungry for wisdom. (*Wisdom* means living our lives in a way that lines up with God's ideas. To be wise, a person needs to know God's ideas and understand how to act on them!)

With joy, God said to Solomon, "Because you asked for wisdom, I will give you more wisdom than anyone else has ever had in the world. You'll be drenched in it! And even better—I will also give you the things you didn't ask for, like money and fame." (No word on the cheeseburgers.) God added, "If you keep following Me like a child follows a parent, I will make sure you live a long time." **Solomon was just a kid, but he was part of God's special plan to bless the whole world.**

Under Solomon's wise leadership, God's people enjoyed life more than ever, and God's house was like a bit of heaven on earth. People far away heard about Solomon's wisdom and said, "Wow! Solomon's God is amazing!"

Sadly, as Solomon grew older and more experienced, his heart began to turn away from the Lord. He surrounded himself with women who followed fake gods. Solomon forgot about the true God and followed the fake gods instead.

Even though God gave him the ability to see the difference between good and bad, had Solomon decided that God wasn't good?

Even though God's ideas make everything better, had Solomon decided that God's ideas were keeping him from good things?

Even though Solomon once had childlike faith, had he chosen grown-up greed instead?

It seemed like it.

Because of Solomon's rebellion, God removed His protection. When Solomon died and his son took the throne, God allowed the kingdom to be chopped in half. Things would never be the same again.

Would there ever be a king who would follow the Lord no matter what? Yes: King Jesus would follow God no matter what.

Dear God,

As I grow, help me to always follow You like a little child. Help me to be hungry for Your wisdom. Amen.

13
Kids Who Grow in Wisdom
Proverbs 1; 31

Throughout the Bible, you'll find words from parents to their kids. These words are important for all of God's kids because they help us grow in wisdom!

Remember Solomon? In his great wisdom, he wrote down lots of words for his kids that are included in the book of Proverbs. He began the book saying,

*My son, be careful to listen to what
your father teaches you. Don't ignore what
your mother teaches. Our words are like a
beautiful necklace or a shiny gold medal around
your neck. They will be a blessing to you!*

The book of Proverbs ends with more words from a parent to a child. This time it's a queen speaking to her son, a prince named Lemuel. He would grow up to be king; and to be a wise, grown-up king, he needed training as a child. Lemuel's mother knew all sorts of things and loved Lemuel very much. She wanted him to be wise, so she taught him wisdom like this:

"There are many things that can pull at your heart and get in the way of doing the right thing. Be careful! Don't forget to be kind and just. Don't ignore people who need your help. Speak for those who cannot speak for themselves."

Lemuel's mom also taught her son something that was important for all kids to know, especially as they grow.

It was about celebrating what God celebrates. For example, the world often celebrates women who look beautiful, but Lemuel's mom wanted to train Lemuel to value what God values: a woman who is wise because she knows and loves God.

To train Lemuel, his mother taught him a poem that went with all the letters of the Hebrew alphabet. That way, Lemuel could know these truths as well as he knew his ABCs. The poem came to a close with some memorable words that are helpful for kids everywhere:

Charm is deceptive
and beauty is fleeting,
but a woman who fears the Lord
will be praised.

What a wonderful man Lemuel would grow up to be if he paid attention to the right things! What a wonderful man Lemuel would grow up to be if he cheered and clapped when he saw someone shape their everyday actions around their worship of God!

You see, in God's family, you don't have to be shiny on the outside to be celebrated. Even the little ways you grow in wisdom are exciting to God! The world may not give you a trophy for working hard at a chore or giving food to someone who is poor, but it all matters to God. So, that's the kind of stuff that matters to God's kids too! When God's kids see one another growing on the inside, they can give one another high fives and wahoos and I-see-you's because they know their Father sees and celebrates this stuff.

When kids have wise parents and listen carefully to their parents' teachings, they find so many opportunities to clap for one another! A parent's wise words are like shiny gold medals around a kid's neck.

These wise words from parents are a gift to all of God's children! (In fact, the whole Bible is made up of wise words from God the Father to His children!) **Kids who grow in wisdom are part of God's special plan to bless the whole world.**

Dear God,

Help me grow in Your wisdom. Help me to see and celebrate wisdom in others. Amen.

14

The Twice-Saved Boy

1 Kings 17

Some powerful people might ignore kids, but God doesn't. He sees and loves every kid, and lots of stories in the Bible prove it! In one story, God saved the same boy twice through His prophet Elijah.

A prophet was someone who spoke God's truth, and God's people were supposed to listen carefully to the prophet's words and believe them. That means prophets had to listen carefully to God.

God told a prophet named Elijah to go to a place called Zarephath. The city was suffering from a drought (which means it hadn't rained in a long time), so food wasn't growing, and people everywhere were hungry—including Elijah! Elijah needed to eat. God told him that He'd commanded a widow (a woman whose husband had died) in Zarephath to feed Elijah.

You would think God would send Elijah to a rich widow who had a giant pantry with an epic snack stash, but He didn't. He sent Elijah to a woman who was struggling to feed herself and her son. When Elijah arrived in Zarephath and asked her for food, she said, "I only have enough flour and oil for one last meal for me and my son. I am going to make this meal, and then we will die." What a scary day for this boy and his mom!

But God had a plan. He sent Elijah to this woman and this boy on purpose. Through the widow, God would save Elijah, and through Elijah, God would save the widow once and the child twice. (Only God can pack so much saving into one story!)

Elijah listened to God and said to the woman, "Don't be afraid. Make a meal for me, and then make something for you and your son. God has promised that your jar of flour and jug of oil will not be empty until it rains again."

The young boy watched weakly as his mother did what Elijah said. As his tummy growled, he probably thought, *Wow! My mom must really believe this prophet's words.* After all, she was giving away their last meal!

He must have been amazed by what happened next. Day after day, the food ingredients did not run out! The boy ate every day and grew stronger. This prophet really had spoken God's truth, and the boy and his mother had incredible proof that God had seen them, provided for them, and loved them. This boy was saved by God—and it wouldn't be the last time.

Sadly, the boy later became ill and died. His mother was devastated! She carried his body to Elijah and cried, "Man of God, what do you have against me?" With great concern, Elijah took the boy and cried out to God three times, begging God to bring the boy back to life. It was an impossible ask, but nothing is impossible with God, right? God listened to Elijah, and guess what? The boy lived again!

When the widow held the twice-saved boy in her arms, she knew Elijah truly was God's prophet. Only the true God would have the eyes to see, the heart to love, and the power to save a boy not once, but twice. **The twice-saved boy was just a kid—but he was a reminder of God's special plan to bless the whole world.**

Every kid can experience God's saving power, although it doesn't always look like we think. Sometimes God doesn't save us from terrible things, but He's offered us saving from the most terrible things: sin and death. God's Son, Jesus, took the punishment we deserve for our sin by dying on the cross. And like the twice-saved boy, Jesus did not stay dead but came back to life through God's power! It's true: any kid or grown-up who looks to Jesus can be saved from sin because Jesus took the punishment, and they can be saved from death because Jesus promised that even when their body dies, they can live forever with Him!

Dear God,

Thank You for seeing me, loving me, and giving Your Son, Jesus, so that I can be saved from the most terrible things, sin and death. Amen.

15
The Good News Girl
2 Kings 5

God wanted kids born into the nation of Israel to learn about Him so that no matter where they were or what they did, they would know God is the true and only God, and they could bless the world with their love for Him. Their parents taught them these important words:

Listen, Israel:
The Lord our God, the Lord is one.
Love the Lord your God with all your heart,
with all your soul, and with all
your strength.—Deuteronomy 6:4–5

If the kids remembered these words, they would grow up knowing that God is most important. They could love Him with all they have, and they could point others to God, since following God is the way to everything wonderful. Kids have always been part of God's special plan to bless the whole world!

When part of Israel was invaded by Syria (one of Israel's enemies), a little girl was captured. The Syrians carried her off so she could work as a servant far away. This had to be very scary for the little girl, yet she knew God was with her. She'd been carried far from home, but she carried the truths of home in her heart.

The little girl began to work as a servant for the wife of a man named Naaman. He was the commander of the Syrian army and a mighty man people deeply respected, but he suffered from a skin disease called leprosy. A person with leprosy was alive, but it was like their skin forgot! Their outsides seemed to rot away and made it hard for the suffering person to be near anyone.

The young servant girl—even though she was so young and so far from home—had compassion on Naaman. The girl remembered a man from her homeland named Elisha who was God's prophet. She told Naaman's wife, "If we were in Israel, I know God could heal Naaman through His prophet!"

For some reason, Naaman and his wife believed this young girl and what she said about God. So, the king of Syria sent a letter to the king of Israel and said, "Naaman is coming so that you can cure him." When the king of Israel read this letter, he was upset! He knew only God could cure something like leprosy, and if Naaman didn't find a cure, Syria might become angry with Israel and make war. But God's prophet Elisha said, "Why are you upset? Tell Naaman to come to me, and then he will know the true God has a prophet in Israel."

When Naaman came, Elisha gave some strange instructions. He said, "Go wash in the Jordan River seven times, and you will be healed." This irritated Naaman. With grown-up pride, he thought, *The Jordan River is no big deal! The rivers in my home country are much better. This is silly.* But Naaman's servants were wise and said, "You should obey God through the prophet."

So Naaman went to the Jordan River. And guess what? After he dipped in the water the seventh time, his skin looked brand-new—as clear and clean as a baby's!

The young servant girl was right. God is the one true God, and following Him is the way to everything wonderful! Naaman had to follow God's words with childlike faith, and suddenly everything terrible on his outsides was made right.

The things the young girl learned about God in her homeland were a blessing for her and for Naaman! **This good news girl was just a kid, but she was a glimmer of God's special plan to bless the whole world.** One day, a Child would come with the best news for sinners: Following God with childlike faith washes us clean from sin! Through Him, everything terrible on our insides can be made right.

Dear God,

You are the one true God! Thank You for sending Your Son Jesus to make us clean from sin. Amen.

16
The Kid King

2 Chronicles 22–24

Because of sin, the nation of Israel broke into two pieces—kind of like when two kids fight over a toy until it breaks in half. (The two pieces, or kingdoms, were called Israel and Judah.) It was a mess! Both nations had lots of kings who didn't love God at all. This was an even bigger mess! Sometimes, though, a king would rule who loved God with all his heart, mind, and strength.

One of these kings was just a kid. His name was Joash, and he became king of Judah when he was seven years old.

The king who ruled before Joash, Ahaziah, hated all of God's ideas. In fact, even though God made mothers to teach kids to love God, Ahaziah's mother taught him to hate God's ideas! When Ahaziah was killed, his death surprised everyone except God, who had a plan to once again replace a king who loved himself with a king who loved God.

Ahaziah's mother was especially upset. When Ahaziah was king, he did whatever she wanted. That meant she'd been secretly running things. Without her son, she didn't have any power. Desperate to rule as queen, she destroyed everyone in the royal family who might've had a claim to the throne. Yikes!

Joash, who was just a baby, was next in line to be king. One of Ahaziah's daughters courageously snuck baby Joash away. She hid him for six years with the priest, Jehoiada. Baby Joash was the true king, but people didn't know it yet.

When Joash was about seven, Jehoiada decided it was time. He built an army of priests and leaders to ensure young Joash could claim the throne as the rightful king of Judah. Together, they conquered the evil queen.

King Ahaziah had listened to his evil mother, but young King Joash listened to Jehoiada, who taught Joash to love the Lord with all his heart, mind, and strength. The kingdom of Judah was peaceful and joyful while Joash was its leader! The people gladly donated their money to restore the house of the Lord (also known as the temple). Through Joash's leadership, the people began to see that following the Lord is the path to everything wonderful! Joash was part of God's special plan, and God's people felt so happy and blessed.

Unfortunately, after Jehoiada died, Joash began to listen to people who did not love the Lord. Joash had wise counsel when he was young. But when he got older, he wasn't careful about who he listened to, and the nation began to turn away from the Lord again.

Joash's story started out hopeful, but he didn't walk in wisdom all his days. One day, though, a Child would come as the one true King. And as He grew, He would follow God with all His heart, mind, and strength. This King would change everything! **Joash the kid king was a hint of the truer and better King Jesus, who was and is God's special plan to bless the whole world.**

Dear God,

Help me know who I should listen to for wisdom and who I shouldn't. Thank You for sending the true King, Jesus! Amen.

17

The Little King Who Loved God's Law

2 Kings 22–23

Joash wasn't the only kid king! A kid named Josiah was crowned king at eight years old. The Bible tells us, "He did what was right in the LORD's sight and walked in all the ways of his ancestor David; he did not turn to the right or the left" (2 Kings 22:2).

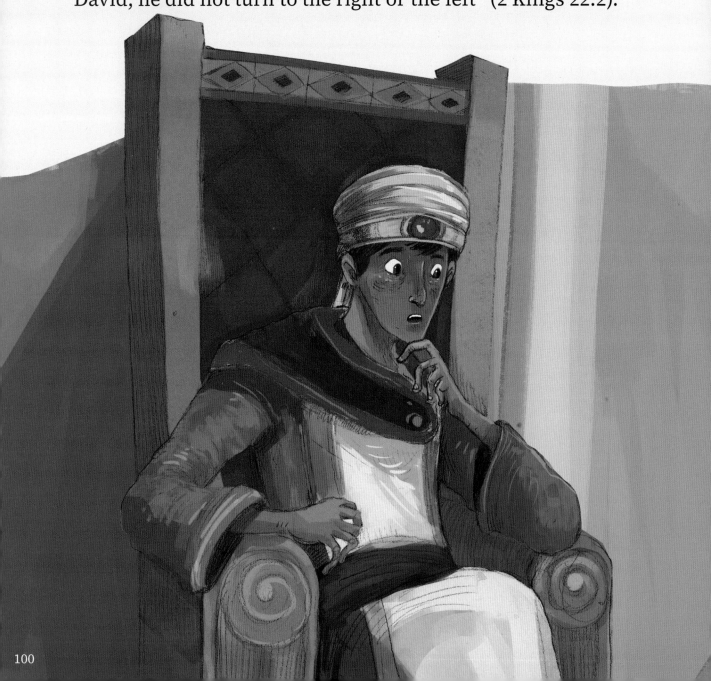

Even though he was just a kid, Josiah loved God with all his heart, mind, and strength, and that affected how he lived and blessed those around him. Like Joash, Josiah used his power to repair the temple. With so many sinful kings who didn't care about God, "the house of the Lord" was often ignored. An abandoned house usually needs lots of repairs!

As Josiah's workers began to repair the temple when Josiah was about eighteen years old, the high priest, Hilkiah, found the book of God's Law. Because previous kings didn't care about God, they didn't care about His Law, and people had begun to forget about the existence of these important scrolls. But when Josiah heard the words written in the newly found book of the Law, he was upset. God's people had not been following God's ideas at all!

Josiah made quick decisions. He told the high priest and some other important workers to talk to God. They immediately went to a prophetess named Huldah, who shared with them God's words. God told them judgment was coming. Sin is a big deal, and it must be punished! But because Josiah was tenderhearted and humble when he heard God's words, God promised the disaster would not come during Josiah's life. Josiah would enjoy peace.

Even though Josiah would not be alive to see the terrible things that were coming, he still wanted to help God's people follow God's Law. He made some important changes, like destroying places where people worshiped fake gods. Josiah also commanded the people to observe Passover, the special day God designed to help His people remember who He was and how He rescued them from Egypt. It was the most wonderful celebration—like the best birthday party of all time! It taught people to look to God to provide for them and rescue them.

In 2 Kings 23:25, some wonderful words describe King Josiah: "Before him there was no king like him who turned to the LORD with all his heart and with all his soul and with all his strength according to all the law of Moses, and no one like him arose after him." This is extra amazing when you think about how young Josiah was! Josiah may have become king when he was little, but his love for God was big, and his decisions helped people follow God. **Josiah may have been just a kid, but he was part of God's special plan to bless the whole world.**

Dear God,

Help me to love You big and to start now, while I'm little. Show me how to help others follow You. Amen.

18

God's Carefully Planned Prophet

Jeremiah 1

God was on the move in the time of Josiah! Remember the high priest, Hilkiah, who found God's Law inside the temple? That was no mistake. God planned for Hilkiah to find the Law, for Josiah to hear the words of the Law, and for the Law to take root inside Josiah's heart so that he could point God's people back to God.

But so much more was happening beyond what people could see! (That's always how it is with God.) Hilkiah had a son named Jeremiah. **Jeremiah was just a baby, but he was an important part of God's special plan to bless the world!** At just the right time, God revealed He had special plans for Jeremiah. God said to him:

> *I chose you before I formed you in the womb;*
> *I set you apart before you were born.*
> *I appointed you a prophet to the nations.*
> —Jeremiah 1:5

God sees, knows, and loves children before their parents ever do—because He is the one who makes children! Even more, God knows every day of a child's life before any of those days happen. Why? Because God is not only the Maker of children—He's the Maker of our days!

Before Jeremiah was ever born, God designed him to tell people God's truth. The job of a prophet might sound easy, but it wasn't! People often hated prophets and closed their ears to their words. After all, God's truth often got in the way of the sinful things they wanted to do, so the people stuck their fingers in their ears and said, "Be quiet! Stop talking!"

Jeremiah knew this, and he was afraid to be God's prophet. He responded to God, "I am only a kid! I don't know how to speak Your truth!" God reached out and touched Jeremiah's mouth, saying, "I have filled you with My words."

From then on, Jeremiah lived as God's prophet, pointing God's people back to God. Jeremiah once described being a prophet like having fire inside his bones! Even if he wanted to stop telling God's truth, the words burned within him. He had to let them out.

Jeremiah shared many difficult messages with God's people during his life. God could see that His people were offering fake worship, mistreating others, and clinging to sin even though sin was (and is) a deadly disease. God's people needed to repent! To repent means to go a different direction. God's people needed to turn from chasing sin and chase after God!

Jeremiah's job was really hard, because God's people didn't want to listen to Jeremiah. They didn't want to live like God's kids, trusting Him to parent them, love them, and lead them. They wanted to lead themselves.

Often, Jeremiah probably thought he wasn't the right guy to be God's prophet. But God made Jeremiah, and God made his days. God knew Jeremiah, and God knew his days.

Every day, God gave Jeremiah His strength so the young prophet could keep following God.

This is true for all of God's children: God made you, and God made your days. God knows you, and God knows your days. Every day, God will give you His strength so you can keep following Him.

Jeremiah once wrote this, and it is wonderful news for all of God's kids!

*Because of the L*ORD*'s faithful love we do not perish,*
for his mercies never end.
They are new every morning; great is your faithfulness!
*I say, "The L*ORD *is my portion,*
therefore I will put my hope in him."
—Lamentations 3:22–24

Dear God,

When things are hard, help me to put my hope in You. I know You made me, know me, and will give me Your strength. Amen.

19
Brave in the Blaze
Daniel 1; 3

Enemies were always coming against God's people—and often, because God's people loved their ideas more than God's ideas, the enemies would win! Even still, some people still loved God with all their heart, mind, and strength.

When people called the Chaldeans invaded Judah, they captured young men who were strong, smart, and handsome. The invaders wanted to undo all these boys knew about God by teaching them Chaldean language, wisdom, and worship. They even changed the boys' names! Three of the boys were named Hananiah, Mishael, and Azariah but the Chaldeans changed their names to Shadrach, Meshach, and Abednego. It was as if the Chaldeans were trying to erase everything that made these Jewish boys who they were! But even though these boys were carried far away from home, they carried the truth of home in their hearts.

The Chaldean king, Nebuchadnezzar, liked to tell people who to worship and how to worship. He made a giant gold statue and commanded, "When you hear music, bow down and worship the gold statue. If you don't, you will be thrown into a furnace filled with fire."

Some of the Chaldeans tattled. "Shadrach, Meshach, and Abednego are not bowing down to worship the statue," they said. "They need to go into the fire!"

Anger flickered across King Nebuchadnezzar's face when he heard this, and he immediately demanded to see the boys. The king growled, "Is it true you don't serve my gods or worship the gold statue? Bow down when the music plays, or I will throw you into the fire! What god could possibly rescue you from my power?"

The boys stood firm. They replied, "The God we serve can rescue us from the fire. But even if He doesn't, we will never serve your gods or worship a gold statue." Even though the Chaldeans tried to make these boys forget their homeland and their faith, they were still filled with God's wisdom. The boys knew God was powerful enough to defeat anything—and they knew they needed to trust God whether He rescued them or not.

Nebuchadnezzar raged and ordered his servants to heat the furnace seven times hotter, tie the boys up, and throw them in the flames. The furnace was deadly hot—so hot that the king's servants were burned up as they took the boys to the furnace!

Bound with ropes, Shadrach, Meshach, and Abednego fell into the furnace. As King Nebuchadnezzar watched to see the flames devour the three boys, he jumped up in a panic. "Didn't we throw three men into the fire? And weren't they tied up?"

Confused, his advisers said, "Yes, of course!"

"Look!" Nebuchadnezzar exclaimed. "I see four men in the furnace—and they're not tied up at all. The fourth man looks like a son of the gods!"

(Who do you think the fourth man was?)

Nebuchadnezzar called out to the boys, "Servants of the true God, come out!" As the boys walked out of the furnace, it was as if they'd never been in there at all. Their clothes looked normal, their hair wasn't singed, and they didn't even smell like fire!

Nebuchadnezzar forgot all about the gold statue. He began to worship the true God. He said, "No other god is able to deliver like this!" He rewarded the boys and started telling everyone what God had done.

Even after being captured and bullied, these three boys knew God was most important. God didn't just rescue these kids—he used their courage to make the king himself tell people everywhere about God! **Shadrach, Meshach, and Abednego were just kids, but they were a part of God's special plan to bless the whole world.**

Dear God,

You are stronger than every scary thing! Give me strength, and help me to love You with everything I have. Amen.

20

The Brave and Beautiful Queen

Esther

After God allowed invaders to enter the Promised Land, God's people ended up all over the place. Their nations, Israel and Judah, weren't really nations anymore, and they became known as the Jewish people. A beautiful young Jewish girl named Esther lived with her older cousin Mordecai in Persia. Esther's parents had died, but Mordecai treated her as a daughter and raised her with wisdom. Esther loved Mordecai and tried to obey him as best she could.

One day, King Ahasuerus of Persia was so angry with his wife that he decided to get a new one. (The king was famous for his quick anger. Being around him was kind of like being around a pile of fireworks ready to explode!) His attendants came up with a plan: they would look all over the kingdom to find the most beautiful unmarried girls, give them months of fancy beauty treatments, and bring them to King Ahasuerus to pick his favorite to be queen.

Beautiful Esther was among the girls brought to the palace. Esther received special care, but Mordecai cautioned her against mentioning she was Jewish. Maybe Mordecai felt this would keep Esther safe. He loved Esther so much! In fact, he visited the palace every day to check on her.

When the king met the young women, he loved Esther more than all the others. He made Esther his queen, put a sparkling crown on her head, and threw a big party for her!

It sounds like everything was going great, but this king was unpredictable. Plus a few other things happened that made the palace dangerous.

For one, Mordecai overheard two guards discussing their plans to kill the king. Mordecai reported the plans and saved the king's life!

And for two, one of the king's officers, an evil man named Haman, hated Mordecai. The king had given orders for everyone to bow down and honor Haman, but Mordecai wouldn't. Haman was furious at Mordecai and all of Mordecai's people, the Jews.

Cunning, tricky Haman told the king about a group of people who weren't following the king's laws. "Wouldn't it be a good idea," Haman suggested, "if you ordered that they be destroyed?"

The king agreed and gave Haman his signet ring. A signet ring was like the king's signature. Anything marked with the ring was an official royal order that could not be changed. And so, Haman sent out letters signed by the king that said all the Jews were to be killed.

When Mordecai and the other Jews learned of the letters, they felt deep horror and sadness. Mordecai sent an urgent message to Esther: "You must go to the king."

Esther was afraid. She wanted to obey her cousin, but she could be killed for approaching the king without permission! Plus, he didn't know she was Jewish. But Mordecai responded to her wisely: "Maybe the reason you have your royal position is to speak up for us."

Esther understood. She said, "If I die, then I die."

Although Esther was young, she was an important part of God's special plan to bless the whole world. Esther and other Jews spent three days fasting from food and drink, and then Esther dressed in her royal clothes and went to see the king—and to see if he would let her live.

Thankfully, King Ahasuerus was delighted to see her!

Esther invited the king and Haman to two banquets. At the second banquet, the king said to Esther, "My queen, you can ask me for anything." Esther bravely said, "King Ahasuerus, I would like for you to save my life and the lives of my people. There is a plan to destroy us."

The king was outraged! "Who would do this?" he roared. Esther replied, "This evil man, Haman."

The king was overwhelmed with anger! How could Haman plan to kill Esther, his queen, and Mordecai, who saved the king's life? The king had Haman killed instead, and he worked with Esther and Mordecai to protect the lives of the Jewish people. From that day on, Mordecai had an important job in the king's court, and the Jews in Persia experienced a wonderful time of peace and joy.

Esther was young, but her story points to another royal leader who was willing to die so that God's people could be saved. Thank You, God, for Jesus!

Dear God,

I know You have placed me in my family, school, and church for a reason. Help me courageously stand up for others wherever I am! Amen.

21

The Promised Child Is Coming!

Luke 1

In the ordinary town of Nazareth lived an ordinary girl named Mary. She was still a teenager, and like lots of girls her age during this time, she was betrothed to be married. *Betrothed* means her parents had promised a man named Joseph's parents that Mary and Joseph would get married one day. It was a serious commitment, and Mary probably thought a lot about what her life would be like with her future husband and future children. That's an ordinary thought lots of kids have: *What will my life be like when I'm older?*

But one day, a not-so-ordinary thing happened to this ordinary girl: an angel came to visit her! His name was Gabriel, and he said, "Greetings, blessed woman! The Lord is with you." When Mary heard this, she felt unsure, overwhelmed, and worried. *Who was this? What did these words mean?*

Gabriel's visit was a big deal. You see, Mary may have looked regular on the outside, but God was going to give her a very special job—one that would change her life (and our lives) forever. **Mary was young, but she was an important part of God's special plan to bless the whole world.**

Seeing Mary's face twist in fear, Gabriel said, "Don't be afraid, Mary! You have found favor with God." "Favor with God" means God loves you and likes you and is kind to you. God's favor can't be earned by being good—favor is given because God is good!

With this reminder of God's goodness, Gabriel continued. He told Mary she would have a son—and not an ordinary son. This Son would be great. Yes, He would be Mary's son, but more importantly, He is the Son of God. He is the King who will reign forever and ever.

Can you believe it? The Child the world had been looking for since that terrible day in the garden of Eden—He was coming! As a Jewish girl, Mary probably knew the story of God's first children. She knew a Child would come one day to bring rescue, but she probably never imagined she would be His mother. Yes, Mary was an ordinary girl, but God wasn't ordinary at all. He invited her to be a part of His incredible plan!

Gabriel told Mary to name the child Jesus, which means, "The Lord saves." This name makes perfect sense. Through Jesus, God would save the world from the enemy of sin by defeating that sneaky serpent forever!

Mary believed the angel. She asked him, "How will this be?" After all, Mary wasn't even married to Joseph yet! But the angel explained that God would place this baby in her womb. What a miracle!

Gabriel told Mary about another miracle: Her cousin Elizabeth, who seemed much too old to have a baby, was going to have a baby too! Gabriel reminded Mary what she knew to be true from the old stories of people like Sarah: Nothing is impossible with God!

Mary took in all this incredible information. Every story she had ever learned about God was pointing to this Child who would change everything! In faith, Mary said, "I am the Lord's servant. May it happen to me as you have said." She loved the Lord with all her heart, mind, and strength!

Mary knew God was good, but she also knew God was not inviting her to do something easy. People probably would not understand what God had asked her to do. They would think she was crazy and not believe she was obeying God! Mary's life would unfold totally differently than she had imagined.

But it would all be worth it. People wouldn't understand, but Mary would know in her heart every time she felt the baby kick—this Child was the ultimate part of God's special plan to bless the whole world. Through Jesus, God would show favor to all who would believe in Him. Thank You, God!

Dear God,

Thank You for Jesus! Thank You that Your favor is not something I can earn. It's something You give through Jesus. When You ask me to do something difficult, help me to answer in faith like Mary. Amen.

22

The Baby Messenger

Luke 1

*A*fter the angel visited young Mary and told her she would be the mother of God's Son, the Child He'd promised since the time of Eve, Mary hurried to her cousin Elizabeth's house. The angel had told Mary that Elizabeth was also miraculously pregnant! Mary couldn't wait to talk to her.

Elizabeth was much, much older than Mary—kind of like a grandma, except that she had never had any children. Like Sarah centuries before her, Elizabeth seemed too old to have a child. But nothing is impossible with God! Sarah's son, Isaac, had pointed to God, and Elizabeth's son would too.

Here's how it all started: Months before the angel Gabriel visited Mary, he came to see Elizabeth's husband, Zechariah, while he served in the temple. Zechariah was a priest, but he'd never seen anything like an angel before! The angel told Zechariah that Elizabeth would have a son, and this son would have an important job: to tell the world about God's Son.

This baby wasn't even born yet, but God already knew him, loved him, and had chosen him as His prophet—kind of like that story about Jeremiah. This baby's name would be John, and John would spend his life sharing one message: "Look! Jesus is coming!"

Sometimes people struggle to understand that a little baby in a mother's womb is an important person, but check out what baby John did when Mary arrived at Elizabeth's house. . . .

Mary walked inside and greeted Elizabeth. Maybe she said something like, "Hello! It's me, Mary!" or "Yoohoo!" or "Anybody home?" Whatever she said, baby John (who was still in Elizabeth's womb) leaped for joy at the sound of her voice! John wasn't even born yet, but he was already doing his job, saying, "Look! Jesus is coming!" It seems his mother Elizabeth believed him immediately.

Elizabeth was overjoyed to know the promised Child was coming—and so was baby John. He jumped up and down

inside his mom when Mary said hello! Elizabeth grabbed her belly and laughed. This baby messenger wasn't even born yet, but he was already great at his job. It was the best news ever: Jesus is coming! Mary began to praise God, singing, "My soul magnifies the Lord!"

Magnifies is a cool word. Have you ever looked through a magnifying glass? When you look through a magnifying glass, you can see things closer and better and bigger! In a way, Mary was singing, "Everything inside me sees the Lord closer and better and bigger—and I am so glad about it!"

And you know what? Baby John's job was to magnify the Lord! He would spend all his days pointing, not to himself, but to Jesus. In fact, when John was a grown-up, he might've felt tempted to make himself seem like a big deal. But he said Jesus must get bigger, and he must get smaller.

Every day of John's life, he pointed to Jesus. And it started before he was born! **Even when John was just a kid, he was an important part of God's special plan to rescue the whole world**—because John would point to the Child who would rescue the world.

Dear God,

Thank You for sending Jesus!
Show me how to magnify You
like Mary and John. Amen.

23

The Change-the-World-Forever Baby

Luke 2

In Mary's womb, baby Jesus grew and grew until finally it was time—the time the whole world had been waiting for since the days of Adam and Eve.

You would think God the Father would have designed it so that this long-awaited King could be born in a fancy, sparkling place—but He didn't do that.

You would think God would have sent Jesus's epic birth announcement to fancy people—but He didn't do that.

You would think God would have given Mary royal robes to dress baby Jesus—but He didn't do that.

God doesn't always do things the way we expect Him to do them, but His way is always more wonderful than we can imagine.

Mary and Joseph lived in Nazareth, but Jesus wasn't born there. The government wanted to count all the people and said everyone had to go to the city that belonged to their family line. Joseph could trace his parents and parents' parents all the way back to King David, so Joseph needed to go to Bethlehem, the city of David.

Mary was really close to giving birth to Jesus. (Sometimes people say things like, "You look like you're about to pop!" but pregnant mothers don't really like to hear that.) Even though Jesus could be born at any minute, Mary still had to make the long journey to Bethlehem.

Unfortunately, Bethlehem was overflowing with people. Too many people! Why didn't God call ahead to make a reservation? Wasn't this His plan?

Mary and Joseph couldn't find a room for people, so they eventually settled in a room used for animals. You won't believe it: after all that waiting, the true King was born right there, next to stinky, loud animals. There wasn't even a crib, so Mary worked with what she had. She wrapped baby Jesus in cloth and placed Him in a manger, which was like a big food bowl for the animals. Wrapping or swaddling was an ordinary thing for a mom to do (you may have seen a swaddled baby before!), but this, of course, was not an ordinary baby.

In the nearby fields, shepherds were watching their flocks while the rest of the world snoozed. Suddenly, an angel appeared to them—looking so bright the shepherds probably wished they had sunglasses—and the angel had the biggest birth announcement of all time:

"Don't be afraid, for look, I proclaim to you good news of great joy that will be for all the people: Today in the city of David a Savior was born for you, who is the Messiah, the Lord. This will be the sign for you: You will find a baby wrapped tightly in cloth and lying in a manger."

Suddenly, this messenger angel was joined by hundreds of other angels! They filled the sky like stars, looking like warriors and singing like a choir. Their voices rang out, "Glory to God in the highest heaven, and peace on earth to people he favors!"

The shepherds just about tripped over their sleepy sheep in amazement. This Savior was for them? This birth announcement was to them? Shepherds weren't fancy guys, and people often looked down on them and didn't trust them. Yet they were favored—not because of anything they'd done to earn the favor, but because God is good and He gave it to them!

The shepherds said, "Let's get to Bethlehem!" and took off running. They soon found Mary and Joseph—and the Baby, just as the angel had said, swaddled and lying in a manger.

The shepherds were overcome with joy. Any baby is a miracle, but this Baby, wow! He would change the whole world! They couldn't help but run around town spreading the good news to everyone. "The Savior is here! The Savior is here!"

Mary watched all of this in awe, thinking over God's goodness in her heart. It was quite an amazing thing to be holding the Savior of the world in her arms. Jesus was still a tiny Baby, but He was God's special plan to bless the whole world.

Dear God,
Thank You for Jesus!
Amen.

24
The Son in the Father's House

Luke 2

Every year, Jesus's parents traveled to Jerusalem for the Passover. (Passover is a big day for the Jewish people. They remember how God rescued them from slavery in Egypt during the time of Moses.)

When Jesus was twelve, His family traveled to Jerusalem for Passover with a bunch of their Jewish friends and family, just like they did every year. But afterward, about a day into their long journey home, Mary and Joseph realized Jesus wasn't with their group! They asked every friend and relative, "Have you seen Jesus?" No one had seen Him.

Everyone probably thought He was with someone else. Panicked, Mary and Joseph went back to Jerusalem to search the city.

Jesus's parents looked for Jesus for three straight days. They must have been worried and confused. Where was Jesus?

If you were a twelve-year-old kid alone in a big, fun city, how would you feel? Afraid? Excited? What would you do? Hide? Find a toy store or a playground? Track down some candy and eat it until your tummy hurt? Mary and Joseph hadn't eaten any candy, but their stomachs probably hurt a lot as they searched for their son.

Finally, they found Him. Jesus wasn't playing on a playground or eating candy or hiding or crying. He was sitting in the temple with important Jewish teachers. He was listening to them and asking questions. The teachers were asking Him questions, too, and they were pretty surprised by His answers. How did a boy so young have such a deep understanding about the things of God?

Years later, Jesus's disciple John wrote something that helps us answer that question. John called Jesus "the Word." He wrote, "In the beginning was the Word, and the Word was with God, and the Word was God" (John 1:1). Yes, twelve-year-old Jesus was a young boy—but He was also God, and He'd always existed! **Yes, Jesus was just a kid, but He is God!**

Jesus is God and is God's special plan to bless the entire world—but it's safe to say Mary and Joseph probably weren't feeling particularly *blessed* at that moment in Jerusalem. They'd been terrified for days as they looked for their son! Mary and Joseph ran to Jesus, and Mary said, "Son, why have You treated us like this? Your father and I have been anxiously searching for You."

Jesus responded in an interesting way. He said, "Why were you searching for Me? Didn't you know that I had to be in My Father's house?"

Mary and Joseph might've thought, *Yes, you need to be with us on the way home to Your father's house right now, young man!* They didn't understand what Jesus meant. Jesus wasn't talking about that house or about that father. He was talking about the temple, which was famously called "the house of the Lord." God the Son was talking about God the Father.

Even though Mary and Joseph didn't understand, Jesus obeyed them, and they traveled home to Nazareth. Like moms tend to do, Mary kept a scrapbook of these memories in her heart. She thought about them often, wondering about this boy who was both her son and the Son of God.

Jesus continued to grow on the inside (becoming wiser) and on the outside (stretching taller). The Bible says He was "in favor with God and with people" (Luke 2:52). That means Jesus pleased God so much—and people liked Him too.

People wouldn't always like Him. One day, people would kill Him, but this, too, was necessary. One day, this young boy would bless the whole world by dying. His death would let sinners become children of God and be in His Father's house forever.

Dear God,

Thank You for making a way for me to be in Your house through Jesus! Help me grow in wisdom like Him. Help me honor my parents like Him. Amen.

25

The Growing Family

John 3:1–21; Ezekiel 36:26–27; Mark 3:32–35; Luke 5

Here's something important to know about God: He is one God, but He is three Persons—God the Father, God the Son, and God the Spirit. (This can be a little confusing. It's okay if you don't totally get it! Sometimes God-stuff can twist our brains into pretzels, but that's okay, because God is good no matter what. And so are pretzels.)

God loves children, and we see can see different angles of God's love from God the Father, God the Son, and God the Spirit!

Jesus is God the Son. Part of Jesus's mission on earth was to make people His brothers and sisters by inviting them to become children of God. God the Father loves kids so much that He invites anyone who wants Him as a Father to become His kids, no matter how big they are!

How does someone become a child of God? A smart religious teacher named Nicodemus came to talk with Jesus about that. Jesus was a grown-up now, and His teachings were full of surprises—like when Jesus told Nicodemus that a person must be born again. Nicodemus was confused! After a person has been born, how can he or she be born again? Is there a big "rewind" button that sends a baby back into his mother's womb? That's weird. Nicodemus was super smart, but this made no sense to him.

But Jesus wasn't talking about being born again through a mother's body. He was talking about being born again through God the Spirit. When a baby is born, that baby inherits lots of stuff from his or her parents, like hair texture, skin color, personality traits—and a sinful heart. A person's heart may beat, but spiritually speaking, without Jesus, a person is dead and needs to be made alive again! God the Spirit can take a person's dead, sinful heart and make it new. When God the Spirit makes our hearts new, it is like we are reborn into God's family. We become God's son or daughter—the truest family there ever could be!

One time when Jesus was teaching, His mother Mary and His brothers came looking for Him. When Jesus's family arrived, people said, "Jesus! Your mother and brothers and sisters are looking for you!" And Jesus said, "Who is my mother? And who are my brothers and sisters? My true family are people who follow God!"

Jesus wasn't being unkind to His family—He was pointing to His truest family. Yes, He had brothers and sisters He had grown up with at home, and to be sure, He loved them very much. But His truest brothers and sisters weren't children of Mary and Joseph—they were children of God, children who had been reborn through God the Spirit!

This message about becoming one of God's children was important, and Jesus wanted the whole world to know. That's why He called twelve different men, saying, "Follow Me!" We call these men "disciples." Their job was to learn from Jesus so they could tell the world about Him.

Let's remember something God said hundreds and hundreds of years before to Abraham: "I am going to give you a big family, and I will bless the whole world through this family!" Abraham's grandson Jacob had sons who became the twelve tribes of Israel, and that family grew and grew. In the same way, the twelve disciples would tell people about Jesus. Those people would be "born again" and become children of God, and God's family would grow and grow!

Spiritually speaking, the disciples were like kids—but they were part of God's special plan to bless the whole world. Through their words, everyone would know about Jesus and how to become a child of God!

Dear God,

Thank You that everyone who wants You as a Father can become Your child because You make their hearts new! Help me to tell others about how to become Your kid. Amen.

26
The Miracle Meal
John 6:1–14; Matthew 14:13–21

Wherever Jesus went, a large crowd of men, women, and children followed. They wanted to hear Jesus teach and to see the miracles He performed. They were amazed by Him! One day, a crowd came, and Jesus had compassion on them. He began to heal anyone in the crowd who was sick.

As the day was ending, Jesus knew it was time for the crowd to eat. He cared about every detail of their lives, so rather than sending them away to eat, Jesus wanted to feed them Himself. Wedged in the middle of this crowd was a little boy who had packed some supper (or maybe his mom had packed it for him). But no one else seemed to think to bring any food. Jesus had a plan in mind, but He wanted to see what His disciples believed about Him. He said to His disciple Philip, "Where will we buy bread so that these people can eat?"

Philip panicked a bit at the word *buy*. How would they ever afford to buy bread for this many people? There were more than five thousand of them! He said, "If we spent all the money we earned for two hundred days, we still wouldn't have enough bread for a crowd this big!"

Then Andrew chimed in. He must've spotted the little boy earlier and knew he had five loaves of bread (probably the size and shape of small tortillas) and two tiny fish. It was only enough food for a kid, but Andrew told Jesus about it anyway. "There's a boy here who has five barley loaves and two fish," he said, "but what good does that do with this many people to feed?"

Of course, Jesus and His disciples didn't take the boy's supper like bullies. They probably asked him if they could have it to feed the people. The boy could've said, "No! This is my supper! Leave me alone!" or "That's silly to think a kid's meal can feed a whole crowd." But it doesn't seem like the boy said anything like that. He just gave up his supper, having faith that it was safe in Jesus's hands.

Maybe the boy had been listening to Jesus's teachings and seeing all His miracles. Maybe the boy wanted to see what Jesus could do with a little lunch. Maybe he didn't really like sardine sandwiches anyway.

Jesus said, "Have the people sit down." Jesus took the boy's loaves and fish, thanked God for them, and began to hand them out to the people. He probably said things like, "Have as much as you want!" and "Are you still hungry? Take more!" The people munched and crunched and munched and crunched. A few people probably even burped. What a delicious feast!

Eventually, the five thousand men (plus all the women and children) had full bellies. "Collect the leftovers so that nothing is wasted," Jesus told His disciples. Although they had started with one small meal, they filled twelve baskets with leftovers—which is probably more than you can fit in your fridge at home! It's funny to think about Philip, carrying all the leftover bread back to Jesus in one big, wiggling pile. He was so worried about bread money!

The people weren't just full—they were amazed. Who was this man who could take a little boy's supper and turn it into an incredible feast for thousands and thousands of people? It's like whatever was given to Jesus somehow became a million times better!

The next day, Jesus began using that feast to teach an important lesson: "I am the bread of life," He said. **The boy with the loaves and fish was just a kid, but he was a part of God's special plan to bless the whole world. His offering pointed to the Bread of Life. Through Jesus, people who were hungry in their souls could finally become full.**

Dear God,

Thank You for sending the true Bread—Jesus! When my soul feels hungry for something, help me to look to You only to fill me up. I know that when I put my life in Your hands, it becomes a million times better. Amen.

27
Jesus Loves Kids
Matthew 18:1–14; 19:13–15; 21:14–16

One day, kids kept coming to Jesus, and the disciples kept trying to shoo them away. They thought Jesus was too important for kids. But they had it all wrong! Jesus told them, "Let the little children come to Me! Don't ever stop them because the kingdom of heaven belongs to children like this." Jesus put His hands on the heads of the little kids standing around Him and blessed them. They knew without any doubt, "Jesus loves me!" To those kids, Jesus's love was better than ice cream, more exciting than a waterslide, warmer and more wonderful than snuggling in a cozy bed.

Other grown-ups didn't understand kids the way Jesus did. When kids saw Jesus's miracles and began to sing songs that He was the Savior, the religious leaders were grumpy. They didn't think Jesus was the Savior, and they wanted the kids to shush! They said to Jesus, "Do you hear what these children are saying?" But Jesus loved the sound and quoted Psalm 8:2, which says that babies will sing praise. Sing it, babies!

Speaking of babies, sometimes Jesus's disciples would act like whiny babies and argue over who was the best. Once they asked Jesus, "Who is the greatest in the kingdom of heaven?"

To answer, Jesus invited a small child to come stand by Him. The little child walked over to Jesus, and Jesus smiled at him with the most wonderful look in His eyes.

Then He said to His disciples, "Unless you become like little children, you won't enter the kingdom of heaven. Anyone who humbles himself like this little child—that is the one who is the greatest in the kingdom of heaven. Anyone who welcomes a child like this, welcomes Me! Anyone who keeps a child like this from coming to Me is in big trouble."

That kid probably felt pretty important and loved that day!

Of course, the disciples might've felt a little confused by all this. Kids didn't seem particularly important to them. Sometimes it seemed like kids were in the way. Their games and ideas and jokes seemed silly compared to "important" grown-up ideas. But Jesus didn't believe kids were in the way, and He didn't look down on kids' ways! In fact, He seemed to say that the kid way is the kingdom way.

Think of it like this: If a trusted grown-up is taking a kid somewhere, a kid doesn't usually say, "Hey, let me drive" or "You have the wrong directions" or "Watch the road, Bucko!" Usually, a kid simply rides along, trusting the grown-up. Kids are great followers! Kids are professionals at trust. When Jesus says to a kid, "Follow Me," a kid is really good at saying, "Sure! I will! Let's go!" When Jesus says to a kid, "I love you," a kid is really good at believing Him.

Adults, on the other hand, can have a hard time trusting. They might say, "Give me the keys," or "Are you sure you know the way?" or "I don't think you really love me" or "Watch the road, Bucko!" Adults have a harder time trusting God because they like to be the boss. They need to become like a kid, willing to trust God to be their Father.

It's kind of cool that even though kids aren't allowed to drive cars or buy plane tickets, they can know the way to God's kingdom. Even if a kid doesn't know how to read a map or a street sign, even if a kid doesn't have a bicycle, even if a kid forgets which way is right and which way is left—that kid can still know the way to God's kingdom! The way is to trust Jesus, and kids are experts at that. **Kids are an important part of God's special plan to bless the whole world.**

And even better, Jesus loves kids. His arms are always open wide to them. If you're a kid, Jesus's message to you is simple and wonderful: "Come to Me."

Dear God,

Thank You for loving me so much! Thank You for wanting me to come to You. Help me to show other kids (and grown-ups!) the way to become a child of God. Amen.

28
The Get-Better Boy and the Live-Again Girl

John 4:46–53; Luke 8:40–56

Sickness and death are some of the scariest things. But one of the best things about God is that anyone who becomes His child will live forever with Him! Yes, God's children will die in this life, but the moment they die, they will be with Jesus and will live with Him forever! Jesus performed two incredible miracles that help us remember that all God's children have life in Jesus.

The first story is about a little boy who became very ill. He was so sick that his family believed he was going to die. They were heartbroken. What could be done for this very sick boy? His father, an important official, was deeply worried about his son and wanted to do whatever he could to make him well again.

The official had heard about Jesus, the incredible man who could heal the sick. People were saying Jesus was in Cana, about twenty-five miles away from the official's home in Capernaum. The official began his journey to Cana, hoping to find Jesus. He was full of faith that this miracle man could heal his precious boy.

Finally, the official found Jesus in Cana and pleaded, "Please come with me to Capernaum and heal my son!" Jesus responded, "Unless you see miracles, you won't believe." Was this man just another person who needed a miracle to believe Jesus was God?

The official begged Him again. "Sir, come down before my boy dies." Jesus said simply, "Go. Your son will live."

The official could have begged again. He could have said, "No! Come with me!" but he didn't. The man believed Jesus's word was powerful enough to heal his son, so he traveled home, trusting in Jesus.

As the man was on his way home, one of his servants met him with great news: "Your son is better!" The official asked, "When did he get better?" When the servant answered, the official realized that was the exact time Jesus had told him, "Your son will live." From then on, everyone in the boy's house trusted in Jesus!

The second story is a lot like the first: the story of another sad father with a sick child. This man, Jairus, was a religious leader with a twelve-year-old daughter who was dying. Like the official, Jairus begged Jesus, "Please come with me to heal my daughter!" Jesus began to walk with Jairus, but on the way to Jairus's home, one of Jairus's servants came to them. He said, "Sir, your daughter is dead. Why bother Jesus any longer?"

Jesus comforted the sad, scared father, saying, "Don't be afraid. Only believe, and she will be saved." In faith, Jairus took Jesus to his home. It was full of loud, crying people mourning the death of this little girl. "Stop crying," Jesus said to them. "She is not dead but asleep."

At this, the crowd started laughing. Who did this man think He was? Could He really not tell the difference between a sleeping person and a dead person? The girl was dead!

Jesus made the crowd leave the house. When they did, He took the little girl's hand and said to her, "Sweetheart, get up!"

And she did. She was alive! Her parents were shocked, but Jesus told them to give her something to eat. After all, alive little girls need lunch.

This little boy and this little girl were just kids, but they were part of God's special plan to bless the whole world! God changed their stories of sickness and death into stories of life—and He does this for all His children. Anyone who follows Jesus will live forever with Him.

Dear God,

I am so glad You are
stronger than sickness and
death! Thank You that Your
children get to live with
You forever. Amen.

29

The Cross: Where God the Father Gave and God the Son Stayed

John 19; Matthew 27:42; Matthew 26:53

"For God loved the world in this way: He gave his one and only Son, so that everyone who believes in him will not perish but have eternal life."—John 3:16

The word *sin* is a word we read often in the Bible. Sin is when we don't believe God's ideas are good and we step outside them. Think about it: God designed people to be kind. When people are unkind, that's outside God's design. God designed people to be truthful. When people lie, that's outside God's design.

Sin is bad in every way. When we are unkind, lie, or go outside God's design in any other way, we hurt others. But we hurt ourselves too. Sin lives in our hearts and shapes us into people who want to run away from God.

Sin is bad for kids. Sin hurts kids. God can't pretend that sin is okay—it's never okay! And so, sin must be punished. God the Father loves kids so much. He would do anything to defeat the sin that hurts kids so much—including sending His Son, Jesus, to take the punishment that kids deserved.

And so, God the Father gave.

That is why God the Son (Jesus) came to live in the world: to die.

Jesus never sinned, and He did so many wonderful things like healing, helping, and teaching people. Even still, some people wanted Him to die. Why? Well, they were mad that He said He was God, and they were jealous that others were following Him.

Those people made an evil plan. They came as a big, angry group, arrested Jesus, and took Him to the leaders who could give permission to kill Jesus. The crowd yelled and yelled at the leaders, telling them what they wanted: for Jesus to die. The leaders could tell Jesus hadn't done anything wrong, but eventually, the crowd seemed so big and angry that the leaders gave in. They said, "Okay, you can kill Him."

The angry people took the Son of God, and they hurt Him, made fun of Him, spit on Him, and nailed Him to a cross. It was the saddest, worst day in the world. As Jesus hung on the cross, the people yelled, "You saved others, so why don't You save yourself?" They knew Jesus had protected others from death, but they laughed, thinking, *He can't even protect Himself.*

But here's the thing: Jesus could have protected Himself. He said, "Don't you know that if I asked My Father, He would send an army of thousands and thousands of powerful angels to help Me?" Jesus stayed on the cross, knowing it was a terrible punishment He didn't deserve but one that the kids He loved did deserve. If Jesus stayed on the cross and endured the punishment, the kids who looked to Him could be saved. They could live instead of die!

And so, God the Son stayed.

Eventually, the sky went dark. Jesus yelled, "It is finished" and took His last breath. The Son of God was dead. His brokenhearted friends took His body and buried Him in a dark tomb, sealing Him in tight with a heavy stone.

Jesus was dead and everything seemed hopeless, but Jesus's death was proof of how much God loves kids. Somehow, even Jesus's death was part of God's special plan to bless the whole world.

Dear God,

I can see that sin is a big deal. Thank You for sending Jesus to take the punishment for my sin. I know You love me so much! Amen.

30
He Is Alive!
Luke 24

Remember how David prayed to God before slinging that little stone at the giant Goliath, and Goliath was defeated? Remember how the three guys were tossed into the fiery furnace but somehow survived and didn't even smell like fire?

God is good at defeating enemies.

Remember how Elijah cried out to God to bring the widow's young son back to life, and God did? Remember when that twelve-year-old girl died, and Jesus took her by the hand? How Jesus whispered, "Sweetheart, get up!" and she did?

God is good at undoing death.

Remember how David wrote about God's plan for all of David's days? Remember how God planned Jeremiah and John the Baptist's lives before they were ever born?

God is good at having a plan.

When Jesus died, Jesus's enemies thought they'd won. When Jesus died, that old serpent thought he'd finally defeated the promised Child. But all the while, God was still God. He was still good at defeating enemies, still good at undoing death—and everything was still going according to His plan.

Jesus's friends came to His tomb early one morning, hoping to care for His body. (Jesus's enemies had treated Jesus's body like He didn't matter, and Jesus's friends wanted to treat Jesus's body with the compassion they'd learned from Him.)

When they arrived at the tomb, the heavy stone was rolled away. What did that mean? They didn't have to wonder for long, because suddenly two shining angels appeared! The angels said, "Why are you looking for Jesus here? Only dead people are in tombs! Jesus isn't dead—He's risen!"

Jesus's friends were shocked, surprised, and stunned! They were startled, amazed, and astounded! They were overwhelmed and overjoyed and over the moon! They were kerfuffled and bamboozled and flummoxed! A gloomy and sad morning had suddenly turned into the best party anyone could have imagined!

Pretty soon, the living Jesus began visiting His friends, and they were able to see that He truly was alive! They could tell this wasn't some faker trying to trick them. This was Jesus. He'd truly died, and He'd truly come back to life.

They saw and touched the scars on His hands and His feet from the crucifixion.

They would never get over this amazing story: Jesus died so that anyone who looked to Him could live and be God's child forever! It was all because God loves kids so much. Jesus died so kids could be God's kids! Jesus died so grown-ups with kid-like hearts could be God's kids! Sin hurts kids, but Jesus took sin's punishment so that those who look to Jesus can have life instead.

But Jesus didn't just die—Jesus lived again! Jesus lives because He is God. Death scares kids, but Jesus took death's meanness so that kids can know that God is bigger than death.

No matter how dark things may seem, God is still God. God is good at defeating enemies, good at undoing death, and good at having a plan. **The serpent thought He'd killed the promised Child—but even that was part of God's special plan to bless the whole world.**

Thank You, God! Jesus is risen! He is risen indeed!

Dear God,

I am so amazed by who You are and what You do! Thank You for being God! Amen.

31
Planting Seeds and Growing Kids
Acts 9:1–19; Matthew 13:1–23; 1–2 Timothy

From the very beginning, God's people were supposed to raise their children to know and love God. Even way back when God's people were about to enter the Promised Land, God very clearly told parents to teach their children about Him. Through the way parents taught their children, God would form a family and bless the whole world!

From the beginning, kids have been like little seeds planted in soil and growing into big fruit trees that make more seeds! Kids would learn about God from their parents, and when they became parents, they would teach their kids about God too. God's family would grow through God's family. Kids have always been part of God's plan to bless the whole world!

When Jesus came, He helped people understand God's family more clearly. Being in God's family wasn't about a kid's earthly parents—it was about whether a kid looked to God as a Father!

When Jesus returned to heaven, it was His followers' job to plant seeds to grow God's family, with the help of God the Spirit. Anytime someone told another person about Jesus and that person began to follow Jesus, that person was a new kid in the family! Other believers could love, help, and teach the new children so that everyone would grow to look more like their Father.

One important "seed planter" in the early church was Paul. Paul was once an enemy of Jesus. He spent his time destroying Christians! But Jesus appeared to Paul, and everything changed. God forgave Paul, made Paul His child, and gave Paul an important job in His family.

From then on, Paul followed Jesus. He dedicated his life to traveling around and telling everyone he could about Jesus. Sometimes his words about Jesus were like seeds that fell on a sidewalk or landed in a thorny bush or got gobbled up by a dog before the seeds could take root. But sometimes, Paul's words about Jesus were heard by someone who could

really hear them, and it was like their heart had good soil! The seed would take root and begin to grow. When this happened, Paul was so excited—there was a new child in the family of God!

One child of God, Timothy, was extra special to Paul. As a boy, Timothy had learned about Jesus from his mother and his grandmother. Because Paul taught Timothy a lot about God, Paul felt like a father to Timothy. Paul spent a lot of time with Timothy, helping him grow to look more and more like Jesus. He loved Timothy so much!

Paul wrote something in a letter to Timothy that is important for all of God's kids to remember, no matter how little or big they are. Paul said, "Don't let anyone look down on you because you're young. Instead, be an example for all of God's kids in the way you talk, the way you act, the way you love, the way you have faith in Jesus, and the way you keep away from sin."

In this way, Paul was a lot like Jesus. He refused to overlook kids or to think they weren't important! He knew God's kids of all ages had an important job—growing to look more like Jesus. The world would know what God is like because God's kids, like Timothy, would show them!

Like Timothy, God's kids might still have lots of growing to do, but they are an important part of God's special plan to bless the world. As they grow, they show the world what God is like!

Dear God,

Thank You for loving Your kids and for giving Your kids an important job—to grow! Help me to grow to look more like You every day. Amen.

32

We Are God's Children!

1 John 3

One of Jesus's closest friends and followers was John. When John met Jesus, John was probably a bit of a stormy dude with a temper problem—maybe like a kid who gets mad and knocks down other kids' block towers. (For example, when John and his brother James got mad at someone being unkind to Jesus, the brothers said, "We should call down lightning from heaven to torch these guys!") Jesus liked to call John and James the "sons of thunder."

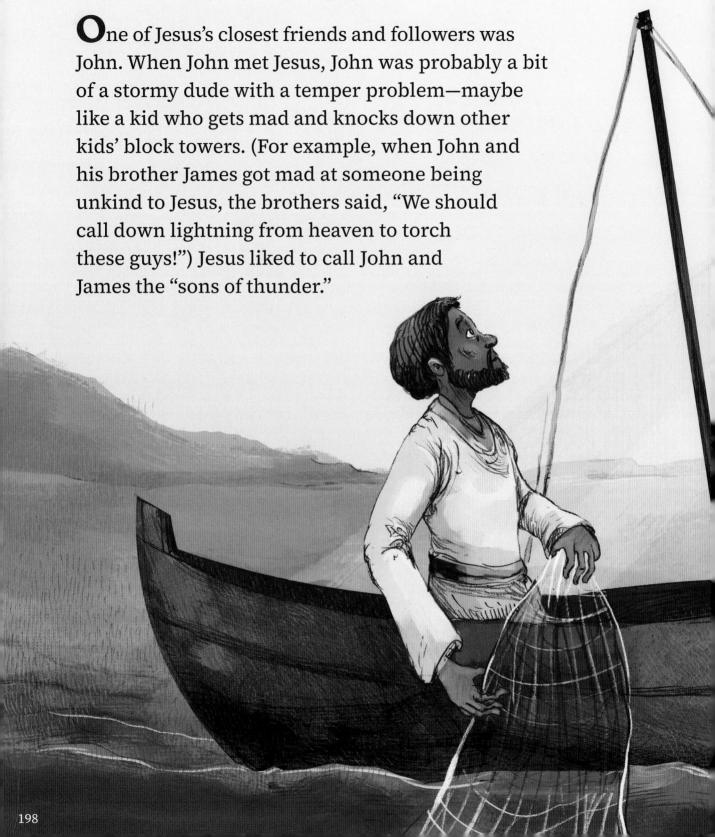

But after walking with Jesus, witnessing Jesus's death, and learning more from Jesus after He came back to life, John was less thundery. He was less like a stormy sea and more like the waters after Jesus said, "Peace, be still!" The more John knew Jesus, the more he grew on the inside!

Forty days after Jesus came back to life, He returned to heaven—but He promised He would send a Helper who would live in the hearts of His people. Soon, God the Spirit came down from heaven and began to live in God's children. Helped by God the Spirit, John began to lead other believers. He became an important leader in the early church, and he wrote a few letters to encourage other Jesus followers.

If you'd known John as a "son of thunder" when he first met Jesus, you'd probably be surprised to hear how he talked in these letters. His voice was full of tenderness. He didn't talk about lighting people up—he talked about loving people! He no longer talked like a "son of thunder" but like a son of God! He wrote, "See what great love the Father has given us that we should be called God's children—and we are!"

John wrote this part like he could hardly believe it, like it was too wonderful for his mind to understand. It's pretty amazing news: Sinners like us should be punished by God. But if we look to Jesus, we get to be God's children forever!

John also wrote about God's love and how it should change the way God's kids treat one another. He said, "Here's what love is: Jesus gave His life for us! We should give our lives for our brothers and sisters. If anyone has plenty of stuff and sees a fellow believer in need but won't share with them, that person doesn't truly love God. You see, we have to do more than say we love our brothers and sisters. We have to actually love them with how we act."

John teaches us that following Jesus means being God's kid—and being God's kid means growing on the inside, becoming more like Jesus every day. It means being wrapped up tight in God's love and freely sharing that love with everyone we know. **In this way, God's kids are a special part of God's special plan to bless the whole world.** God's kids get to rejoice every day that they are in His family!

Dear God,

Thank You for building such a wonderful family! Help me to love others the way You have loved me. Amen.

33

Good News for God's Kids
Revelation

Even though John was the disciple Jesus called "son of thunder," John grew up to be a strong, gentle leader of the early church. Becoming God's kid changed John's life. As he grew on the inside, he began to look less like a son of thunder and more like a son of God!

Of course, that didn't mean John never got in trouble. Kids get in trouble for not following rules—but sometimes God's kids get in trouble because they follow Jesus! Some people don't like God, so they don't like His kids. Jesus's disciples got in lots of trouble for following Him, and John was no different.

Near the end of John's life, when he was in trouble yet again for following Jesus, God gave John a vision of some important truths from Jesus and a sneak peek of things that would happen in the future. This was such a blessing to John and the rest of God's kids. Jesus's words and promises helped them keep going when life felt extra difficult!

John wrote this vision down in a letter to churches, and his words are now the very last book in the Bible: Revelation. Revelation has lots of important words from Jesus for God's children. The main message is really good news for God's kids: Jesus is reigning in heaven right now, and He will come back one day as a forever King.

Can you imagine how wonderful that sounded to God's kids, like John, who were being mistreated back then for following Jesus? Or how wonderful it sounds to God's kids today who are mistreated for following Jesus? God is coming to get them! Soon, they will be at home with Him!

Ever since John wrote his letter, God's kids have been excited about Jesus coming back. Whenever life gets hard, God's kids can remember, *Jesus is coming soon, so I will keep going!*

Jesus told John lots of things that God's kids need to know as they live in a world full of sin and the serpent's tricks. Jesus told John stuff like this:

- God's kids need to look to their Father and not be tricked by that serpent. God will bless them for this!

- God's kids need to be on guard against sin. God will bless them for this!

- God's kids need to be prepared to get in trouble for following Jesus. God will bless them for this!

Living this way is hard, but that's why God's kids have the Holy Spirit to help them. The Holy Spirit is a Helper and a promise—a promise that Jesus will come back.

When Jesus comes back, God will do several important things:

- God will fully destroy the great enemy of God's kids: that serpent.

- God will totally wipe out the thing that hurts kids the most: sin.

- God will make a new home for His children. It'll be a place where only wonderful things can happen. It'll be a place where there will be no more crying or pain or death. Most importantly, it'll be a place where God's children can be with God forever!

For God's kids, that day will be the most exciting day in the world! It'll be like a surprise party, a trip to a theme park, an all-you-can-eat buffet, and a family reunion crammed into one epic celebration! We'll finally be with our forever Father and our forever family in a forever home that is forever wonderful.

John ends his letter with words that God's kids cry out whenever life feels hard. He wrote, "Come, Lord Jesus!"

It's really true—Jesus is coming. One day, God's kids will be with Him forever. Until then, God's kids can pray like John, "Come, Lord Jesus!" and they can tell the world about Jesus. After all, Jesus is the best news in the world, and kids are great at sharing good news. **Truly, God's kids are an important part of God's special plan to bless the whole world.**

Dear God,

Thank You for the promise that Jesus is coming back! When it is hard to follow You, help me remember that promise. I am so glad that Your kids will be home with You forever one day! Amen.

The Story of the Child

As you may have noticed from the little stories in this book, the Bible tells one BIG story. The Bible's big story teaches us about God's plan to rescue a sinful world by sending His Child, Jesus, to make the way for all who look to Him to become children of God. That's right—the Bible's big story is a story about kids! (We told you kids are part of God's special plan to bless the whole world!) So, as an extra treat, here's a retelling of the big story.

Back in the beginning, there was nothing. No playgrounds and no pancakes. No salamanders and no swimming pools. No bees or beads or beans or beets.

There weren't even any kids! But there was the best Parent in the world: God. So God made the world. He made lights and land and oceans and plants and animals.

And then God made kids. Well, they were probably more like grown-ups, but they were also brand-new to the world, so that makes them a lot like kids too. God loved them so much and wanted to teach them to grow to be more like Him. That makes them like God's kids.

God lived with Adam and Eve in the most wonderful home, the Garden of Eden. Everywhere they looked there was something fun to do and something delicious to eat. Most of all, God was what made the place wonderful.

God gave one rule: They could eat from every tree except one. One tree was off limits.

But one day, a snake approached. He told Adam and Eve they should ignore God's rule and said God was keeping them from something good. (That doesn't really sound like God, does it?)

Terribly, Adam and Eve listened to the snake and broke God's rule. Suddenly, they wanted to hide from God. They felt embarrassed and angry at one another. When they disobeyed God, it was like saying, "I don't want to trust You, God." This is called sin, and sin ruined everything.

Because of their sin, Adam and Eve had to leave their wonderful home, but God sent them away with a promise. One day, a woman would have a Child, and that Child would beat that sneaky snake for good and rescue God's children.

Adam and Eve had kids, and their kids had kids, and their kids had kids, and their kids had kids . . . until the world was full of people. But none of them seemed like they could beat that sneaky snake. In fact, they all seemed to listen to him. When God made a rule to keep all these kids safe and help them be kind, they hated it—and sometimes they even hated God. They forgot He was the best Parent in the world!

Sometimes kids look like their parents on the outside, and that's fun. But the world was full of kids who looked like Adam and Eve on the inside—full of sin—and that wasn't fun at all! Who could rescue them?

God would.

Here's something extra wonderful about God: God is God the Father, God the Son, and God the Spirit.

This is hard for even the brainiest grown-ups to understand, but here's the most important part for our story:

God the Father sent God the Son as a baby who would grow up to beat that sneaky snake for good.

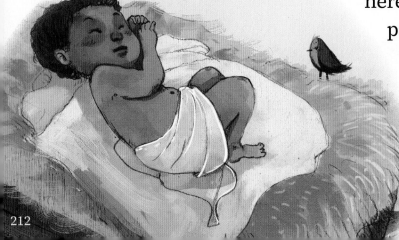

In lots of ways, Jesus is like us! Jesus was born like you were born. He was a kid like you. Grown-ups had to help Him learn to walk and talk. He giggled and played. He probably skinned His knees and enjoyed His favorite snacks.

In one important way, Jesus is not like us. He never sinned. He is the only person in the whole world to do this!

Some people loved their sin so much that they became angry with Jesus. They pretended He was a criminal who needed to be punished. Even though it wasn't fair, Jesus was arrested and killed.

It was the worst day—but it was also part of the plan to beat that sneaky snake for good.

When Jesus died on the cross, it was a punishment. But it wasn't Jesus's punishment—it was the punishment that sinners deserve. Everyone who'd listened to the sneaky snake and disobeyed God could look to Jesus and get forgiveness since Jesus had taken their punishment! God the Father will forgive anyone who looks to God the Son.

But the news gets even better. When God forgives our sin through Jesus, we become God's new children! Something incredible happens: God the Spirit comes to live in our hearts, and God begins to be our true Parent, reminding us of His love and teaching us to live like Him.

But the news gets even better. Jesus didn't stay dead! God the Son beat that sneaky snake for good, and He came back to life. Soon, Jesus returned to heaven, where He is right now, ruling as a king. He is like our big brother, asking God to help us when we need it and sending God the Spirit to live in the hearts of all God's children.

And guess what? The news gets even better. One day, Jesus will come back and gather together all of God's children! He will set up a new and wonderful home where we will be together with God forever.

Am I a Child of God?

Kids are great! Yes, YOU are great. When God thought of you, He had a great idea, and when God made you, He did a great job. God made you on purpose, shaping you to be the you-est you—and we are so glad. Look in the mirror sometime and say, "Hey you! God made you! Thanks, God!"

But that's not the only thing that's important to know about you.

Did you also know that you're a sinner? That all kids are sinners? That all people are sinners? A sinner is a person who sins. But what is sin? Sin is when we think, *I'm going to do what I want instead of what God wants.*

For example, it's God's idea for us to be kind to our brothers, sisters, friends, and everyone else. When we do, say, or think something unkind, we sin. Sin is natural to us! No one has to teach kids to grab a toy and say, "Mine!" They just know how to do that. Sin is as sneaky as a snake, seeming to be a good or fun thing at first and then turning poisonous.

Sometimes we say, "Okay, I will never sin again!" and we use all our muscles and try as hard as we can and think we almost got it until . . . oops. We sin again. No matter how hard we try, we can't fix ourselves. We need a Fixer, a Rescuer, a Sin-Squasher.

That's why Jesus came. He lived the perfect life that none of us could live. He died the punishing death that we deserve. And He came back to life—showing us that when we look to Him, we have new life too! Not only that, but when we look to Jesus, we become children of God. God's kids!

What does it mean to "look to Jesus"? It doesn't really have anything to do with your eyeballs. You don't need glasses or a telescope to look to Jesus. Looking to Jesus is something that happens inside you. It goes kind of like this:

- God helps a kid see that he or she is a sinner who needs rescue.

- The kid realizes and honestly admits, "I am a sinner! I need help! I cannot do it!"

- The kid looks to Jesus as his or her only hope for rescue from sin.

- In love and delight, God welcomes this kid to be His kid forever and ever!

And this begins a life-long journey of growing as God's kid. God's kids have God's help to fight sin. Of course, we will still sin, but slowly, we will grow to look more and more like Jesus. It's kind of like the height chart at the doctor's office. We'll look back and say, "Whoa! I am slowly becoming kinder!" or "Whoa! I am slowly growing in patience!" It might feel like a snail's pace sometimes, but it's always a miracle. Thank You, God!

Now What?

You may want to spend some time thinking and praying about all this stuff. God is never mad when we ask genuine questions or try to understand Him! Maybe you'd like to find a grown-up who loves Jesus and loves you and ask that grown-up some questions. That's a great idea, and your grown-up will be glad to talk to you.

On the other hand, you may be honestly thinking, *I know I'm a sinner, and I want to look to Jesus!* You can pray right now. God hears you! Tell Him what you're thinking and feeling, and ask Him to rescue you from sin and make you His kid forever. It doesn't matter what words you use because God hears you, understands you, and loves you. If you do this, be sure to find a grown-up who loves you and loves Jesus and tell them. Your grown-up will be glad to talk to you and help you understand more.

By the way, God's kids have lots of awesome help for growing. God the Spirit is with you always, and He will comfort you and remind you of what is true. He especially does this when we read the Bible, which is the same as God talking to you. You can pray, which is another way of talking with God. God will always listen to you! Plus, there's this: Because God is your Father, anyone who truly loves Jesus is your brother or sister. You have a huge family of people to help you grow!

Your Story of Being God's Kid

Have you looked to Jesus to rescue you from your sin and to make you God's child forever? If so, you're God's kid! When God's family grows, it's a miracle—and heaven has a party. In fact, Jesus said this: "There is joy in the presence of God's angels over one sinner who repents" (Luke 15:10).

So here's your chance to write your celebration story. Grab a notebook or a piece of paper, and write whatever you want. On the next page are some questions if you need help. You don't have to know the answers to all of these—they are just here to get your brain going. Your story is wonderful, no matter how you tell it!

- When did you realize you needed Jesus?

- What were you thinking about? What were you feeling?

- Were there any Bible verses or other books that helped you realize this?

- Is there a person or two who has helped you know about Jesus and helped you want to follow Jesus?

- Have you noticed anything different in your heart and mind now that you are following Jesus?

- How do you think you will grow on the inside because of Him?

- What makes you the most excited about being God's kid?

I'm God's Kid!

Here's my story:

_____

_____

_____

_____

_____

_____

_____

_____

_____

_____

_____

_____

_____

_____

_____

_____